ALSO BY TERESA GRANBERRY

God is in the Details, Volume 1

God is in the Details, Volume 2, Tweens Version

God is in the Details, Volume 3, Holiday Version

THE SECOND TO THE LAST BOX

FINDING JOY AND PURPOSE IN MIDLIFE AND BEYOND

Teresa Granberry

Harvest Creek Publishing

WILLIS, TEXAS

Copyright © 2019 by **Teresa Granberry**.

All rights reserved. No part of this publication may be reproduced, distributed or transmitted in any form or by any means, including photocopying, recording, or other electronic or mechanical methods, without the prior written permission of the publisher, except in the case of brief quotations embodied in critical reviews and certain other noncommercial uses permitted by copyright law. For permission requests, write to the publisher, addressed "Attention: Permissions Coordinator," at the address below.

Unless otherwise noted Scriptures are taken from *The New International Version* of The Holy Bible.

Scripture quotations marked (NKJV) are taken from the *New King James Version*. Copyright © 1979, 1980, 1982 by Thomas Nelson, Inc., Publishers.

Teresa Granberry/Harvest Creek Publishing
10891 Dauphine
Willis, Texas 77318
www.harvestcreek.net

Cover and Book Layout ©2019 Harvest Creek Design

Ordering Information:

Quantity sales. Special discounts are available on quantity purchases by corporations, associations, and others. For details, please contact teresa@harvestcreek.net.

The Second to the Last Box/Teresa Granberry. —1st ed.

ISBN 978-0-578-55857-8

To Sam, my husband, and my best friend

*How blessed I am to spend life with you. Every day is a gift full of love, laughter, and kindness with you walking by my side.
You are the love of my life.*

To Justin, Lauren, Misty, and Tyler

You inspire me to be a better Mom and a better person. Thank you for reflecting God's goodness on this earth. May the legacy I'll one day leave behind equip you to find unparalleled success in all you do. I love you.

ACKNOWLEDGMENTS

YOU'VE HEARD IT SAID that everyone has a book in them. And while that may be true, actually retrieving a book *out* of a person takes the love and support of others. God's most generous gifts to me have been the devotion of my husband, my children and grandchildren, and the many dear friendships made throughout my life. The encouragement from family and friends has been the impetus to complete this project, and for that, I am grateful.

After realizing that the theme of this book was a more prevalent issue than expected, I launched a national survey to obtain additional input. Those who responded are people I don't know personally, but who share a collective hope that their lives on earth will count for something important. Thanks to them for being willing to share their stories, and for demonstrating that we can be useful in making a difference, at any age.

Most importantly, all praise goes to my Lord and Savior Jesus Christ who believes in me and has a perfect plan for my life. To Him be the Glory, today and always.

CONTENTS

Acknowledgments vi
Foreword ix
Preface xiii

PART ONE
Who Put Me in A Box?

CHAPTER 1: Peddle On Through the Curves......................19
CHAPTER 2: Will Someone Let Me Out of Here? 25
CHAPTER 3: The Great Contradiction 33
CHAPTER 4: What the Research Says About Our Boxes....41
CHAPTER 5: Middle Age or Middle Malaise 47

PART TWO
Generational Mindsets

CHAPTER 6: Labels We Place On People 53
CHAPTER 7: What's In That Box?..59
CHAPTER 8: What We Each Have and What We All Need .69
CHAPTER 9: Service or Serve Us...79

PART THREE
Do I Really Belong in Here?

CHAPTER 10: You Aren't Done Until You're Finished.......85
CHAPTER 11: Retired? Or Just Plain Tired 89
CHAPTER 12: Act Your Age...93
CHAPTER 13: Our Biggest Concerns From the Top
             of the Hill..99

PART FOUR
We Are Breaking Out of Here

CHAPTER 14: Live in the Now 109
CHAPTER 15: Retire To Something 115
CHAPTER 16: Never Stop Learning 119
CHAPTER 17: What To Do When You're Feeling Old 125

PART FIVE
Life Outside of a Box

CHAPTER 18: Mentoring Them for Success 137
CHAPTER 19: Prepare to Leave a Legacy 143
CHAPTER 20: Mapping Out the Next Ten Years 149
CHAPTER 21: Doing the Old Things in a New Way 157

CONCLUSION

The Passing On of Wisdom 165
Where Do You Go From Here? 171
A Prayer of Blessing for Middle Age 173
About the Author 175

FOREWORD

IT HAS BEEN MY DISTINCT PLEASURE to know Teresa and Sam Granberry for the last thirty-plus years. I have seen how they have grown and developed both spiritually and professionally over the previous three decades.

Therefore, it does not surprise me that Teresa has written this book. They have always chosen to '"live in the present, not in the past." They are both prime examples of what this book is all about.

That is, to live in the present, to assess and reassess your God-given strengths and talents. The importance of knowing that different seasons of life may call for different skills, knowledge, and abilities.

This book emphasizes that you must always apply yourself in ways that maximize your opportunities in your current season of life. Don't look to the past, look ahead!

Ecclesiastes 3:1-2 states, "There is a time for everything and a season for everything under heaven." Verse 11 says, "He has made everything beautiful in its time." And Teresa encourages you to not run ahead of God, but also not to run behind God. Walk with God in His perfect timing for all of your pursuits.

Teresa challenges the reader to not allow others to put you in a specific mold, or box, but to learn to think outside the box and believe all things are possible through God. When God said in Jeremiah 29:11, "For I know the plans I have for you", declares the Lord, "plans to prosper you and not to harm you, plans to give you hope and a future," He didn't mean this until a certain age in your life, but for your entire life!

This book is full of examples of people who made their greatest achievements in life when they were in their 50's, 60's, 70's, and 80's. It is not too late for you to get a new passion, or new desire to accomplish what may have been in your heart your entire life. Teresa challenges the readers to trust God for direction, knowledge, and wisdom to complete what is God's assignment for you as you progress in your chronological years on the earth.

1 Corinthians 13:11 says, "When I was a child, I talked like a child, I thought like a child, I reasoned like a child. When I became a man, I put childish ways behind me."

This book states that different stages of life require different ways of using our skill sets. What worked for us as a child or teenager will no longer work for us in our 20's and 30's. So, we have to be creative in our thinking and learn new coping skills to prepare us for our present.

As you read this book, you are encouraged to not look back on your failures or mistakes, or poor decisions in your life, but to look to the present. God is a now God! Isaiah 43:18 says, "Forget the former things, do not dwell on the past. See, I am doing a new thing." Teresa states that we are all capable of doing far more than we ever dreamed, especially in our older, more mature years. Don't count God out and don't count yourself out. The present years of your life could be your finest moments, your greatest days. May you, as a reader, be encouraged to believe that God wants to do momentous things in your life.

I encourage you to read this book, be encouraged and inspired by it, ignite the dreams and desires within you that have been lying dormant to come to fulfillment!

James F. Allen, M.Ed. (Counseling)
Lic. Prof. Couns., Supv.
Lic. Marr. And Family Couns.
Lic. Chem. Dependency Couns.
Certified Sexual Addiction Couns.
Mediator (Civil and Family); Lic. and Ordained Pastor

FOREWORD

GROWING UP IN ZAMBIA, we had a community center where we played basketball or stopped for cold Fanta® or Coca Cola®. One of the community walls was a bulletin board with news and some quip on life. One that sticks to memory, and bears on the topic at hand, read:

> *If a man is not handsome at 20, strong at 30, rich at 40, and wise at 50, he will never be handsome, strong, rich, or wise.*

As much as we love the neat boxes of milestones, there is no one-size-fits-all. I've taken the most scenic route to my career as a Performance Psychologist and defied odds as well as stereotypes to get there. Along the way, I've been blessed to have Teresa as a guide, companion, and confidante; the concepts and stories she has shared in our private conversations as well as in this fantastic book have positively shaped my family and me.

This book is written in a simple, easy-to-understand way and transports the reader to the scenes within her storytelling—it is easily *relatable*. I saw myself in some of her stories and experiences, even at my age (on April 20, 2018, soon after my 40th birthday, I became a proud AARP member).

Teresa underscores a key value of mine: *age with grace*. I want to age like grapes and become a wine that complements joyous meals rather than aging like milk. In *The Second to the Last Box*, you will find yourself challenged and discover that, to age like grapes, you have to get stomped.

No, Teresa doesn't tear you down; on the contrary, she shows you how to crush the vanity, battle the insecurity, and release your greatness every day of your life. With vulnerability and humor, Teresa weaves a tale of living life to the full and contributing meaningfully to the very end.

Dr. Kozhi Sidney Makai, PhD., PsyD
Performance Psychologist & Author
Kozhi Makai Worldwide

PREFACE

Courage is being yourself every day, in a world that tells you to be someone else.

LET ME BEGIN BY SAYING, I don't like boxes. As a pastor's daughter, my family and I moved every few years because my father would be appointed to a new congregation. It was always a little unnerving to walk in from school and notice stacks of cardboard containers scattered around. Seeing that image meant we would soon be leaving the familiarity of our home and heading somewhere new. Everything we owned would be packed up tightly and shipped off to another destination. Consequently, my perception of boxes as a kid wasn't always pleasant.

Boxes come in many forms to accomplish their purpose. For example, there is the penalty area on an ice hockey rink (a.k.a. the "sin bin") or the set of brackets placed next to multiple choice answers on a survey (a.k.a. the "checkbox"). Be it figurative or literal, the primary purpose of a box is to contain or to confine something.

At times we use boxes to remove excess clutter when space is needed. You grab a container, gather up the overflow, and set it aside for a donation or to give away. And then there are boxes that store items like Christmas ornaments or seasonal clothing that will only be used on a limited basis. We carefully label these cartons so that if, or when the time comes, we may easily retrieve their contents once more.

Can you imagine placing *people* in boxes? That sounds preposterous, at least in the physical sense. But that's what we do as a society when we group people based on age, stage or any distinguishing characteristic which presumes to define them. And we put labels on these human boxes like blue-collar, white-collar, student, graduate, rookie, veteran, or senior. People are lumped into commonly known units intended to characterize them. So, I'll rephrase my question: Should individuals be stereotyped or branded with a label or characterization like physical items stored in containers?

To me, the answer is "no." We should not put people into boxes. Personally, I don't want to be confined, contained, or set aside for later. And I don't want to be considered "overflow," when my friends and loved ones mentally stow me away until needed.

Sadly, when we overgeneralize people by age and stage, it creates separation and division, rather than unity and commonality. When we partition people, based on what we do, where we're from, or any other limiting criteria, we fail to learn *from* and grow *with* each other.

So, you might ask, why did I write a book about boxes if I don't like them? Good question. A few years ago, the world tried to put me in a metaphorical box. Emphasis on the word *tried* because I'm a tough nut to crack. After unfortunate circumstances, that quite frankly were beyond my control, I began to sense that my experience, talent, and expertise were no longer relevant to the world. It felt like I was being sent out to pasture to graze until my time on the earth was done.

Done. Now there's another concept I struggle with. Is the purpose of any living, breathing human ever *done*? We will talk more about the use of this word in another chapter. But for now, I like what the American writer Richard Bach said, "Here is the test to find whether your mission on Earth is finished. If you're alive, it isn't."

Throughout my life, it has been rewarding when the Lord directed a significant change for me. In every step and every stage, God has given me purpose. And ultimately in the end when He shows me that it's time to stand beside still waters and restore my soul, so be it. When He says, "Your purpose on Earth is complete," I will rest assured that the race is over.

But when the *world* dictates how I am to live out the remainder of my days as a person growing older—well that's another matter. That is when I feel that I've been put into a box!

A few years back, I was rejected because of my age (and mind you an age I didn't consider to be *that* old). Soon after, I determined to become a voice for those facing the insurmountable giant called "aging." Statistics show that approximately twenty-five percent of the U.S. population is age 55 and over. Around 7000 people a day turn sixty-five. There's a reasonable probability that thousands of people have already faced or will soon be confronted by the same prejudices as me when it comes to their age.

Utilizing the benefits of social media, I launched a national survey to assess the significant concerns of people at midlife or older. Hundreds of people responded, sharing their thoughts, personal stories, and apprehensions regarding growing old. It was shocking to read of the rejection so many had encountered. A few of their stories made my own situation pale in consideration!

You may have heard the adage, "growing old isn't for wimps." And that's true. In this day and time, people in their middle and older years must be stronger and braver than ever. The world is moving at a tremendous pace. Technology evolves so rapidly that by the time you figure out how to use your new phone, it's practically obsolete!

Life moves fast. And you can't be feeble, hoping time will slow down for you to catch up. Don't be stuck in a world that once was. Life must be lived in the here and now.

Middle-aged people need to stay educated. We need to be informed about what *is* and what is yet to come. We need the determination to preserve our health, our minds, and our finances.

This book outlines the societal boxes used to segregate us, and it addresses our collective fears. Throughout these pages, we'll explore relevance, purpose, and the challenges facing a person as they pass through middle age and then move into retirement. We will debunk a few common misconceptions about aging and living out our last days. You'll read numerous instances of people who have lived their most exceptional days in the second half of life, during a time the world deemed their *final* chapter.

It's funny to admit, but after all of this research and study my personal opinion of boxes has begun to change; I now view them optimistically. It equates to those cartons left on the front porch, delivering the merchandise you ordered online. You know—the packages that display a *smile* on the side of the box. They are routinely filled with items that are fun, useful, or important. Life in your later years can be like that, too, filled with exciting gifts and long-anticipated blessings.

Let's embrace the positive opportunities you can only experience later in life. May this book open your mind and heart to the exciting possibilities awaiting a person who has lived for *more* years on the earth, than they have yet to remain. Be encouraged to learn that your greatest days are ahead. Realize that you are not defined by, nor constrained by age, stage, or any other limiting criteria.

As many can attest, your best life begins in the second-to-the-last box!

Teresa Granberry

PART ONE

WHO PUT ME IN A BOX?

CHAPTER 1

PEDDLE ON THROUGH THE CURVES

Life moves pretty fast! If you don't stop and look around once in a while, you could miss it. FERRIS BUEHLER

IT'S A LITTLE AWKWARD TO ADMIT that one of the most powerful quotes in my life toolbox came from a movie about a rebellious teenager who played hooky from a day of school. But Ferris Buehler learned more out on the street during his infamous "day off" than he ever would have in a classroom. And in the words of this teenage philosopher: Life. Moves. Fast.

Perhaps I should have engraved this quote onto my forehead when I was Ferris' age. Think of all the opportunity that gets wasted in adolescence. Does any young adult think about how fast their life is moving? I certainly didn't!

When I was a teenager, there were two distinct thoughts I had toward older people. And by older people, I meant anyone that was forty and over. These were people who had raised their children, worked for years in a career, owned a beautiful home, or accomplished something significant with their life.

My perspective at that time viewed people over forty as *ancient*. There was a significant gap between the start of their life and that of mine. My grandpa confirmed this every time he began one of his many stories with, "Back in my day" or "When I was your age." The thought of becoming 40, 50, or even 60 years old was so distant, it was unimaginable.

Additionally, I perceived the lives of these ancient people as *huge*—not in physical stature, but as larger-than-life giants. Their responsibilities, their quests, and the recollections of their pilgrim's journey seemed colossal. My grandfather's tales centered around him being gassed in Germany during the world war and about his escape to a safer land where he could start a family. Listening to Grandpa's heroic quests made me feel like I was viewing a summer blockbuster.

My world back then was small and manageable. My parents handled everything necessary for me to exist. Responsibility meant simple tasks like feeding the dog, doing my homework, clearing the table, and putting my laundry away. To even consider having a career, raising a family, or managing any other major life event was far from my mind.

But life moves fast. I'll never forget the day my view of age and responsibility changed. My parents had loaded the car with all my worldly belongings, and we were headed off to a college, three hours away. Earlier that morning, I found my Mom measuring the window in my room at home. She mentioned that she was "re-doing" the space since I was moving out, and it would become a sewing and craft area. But Mom cautioned that there was "no need to worry" because she would leave a bed in there to accommodate visitors. This all seemed a little strange, and it never dawned on me that I would be a guest in their home from that day forward.

When we arrived at the dorm, my parents carried boxes and furniture up to my new room. After everything was unloaded, we grabbed a meal at a local restaurant. Mom reached into her purse and pulled out an envelope containing paperwork for a checking account.

"This is your college savings plan; we're giving you ownership of the funds. Of course, you'll want to manage this well because we won't be paying for your expenses any longer," Mom advised.

"Wait. What?" I asked. Granted, I can be slow to catch on, but it seemed like I was being kicked out.

"Every mother bird prepares their babies to leave the nest one day. Well, I'm the mother, and you're the baby bird. I'm kicking you out of the nest." Mom was always a get right to the point kind of parent. And I was certainly getting the point. They *were* kicking me out! And it was a little painful.

"I'm not ready to fly," I said with a slight panic in my voice, flapping my arms in protest.

"Yes, you are, and you'll be fine. Spread your wings and do it," Mom confidently replied. I glanced over at my stepfather, who was nodding his head in agreement.

From that day forward, I never lived again in their home, nor relied on my parents to make decisions regarding my care. During a couple of spring and summer breaks, I was a guest in that sewing room, making sure to return everything to its place before heading back to *my* home at college.

Life moves fast. Soon I was married, with children and a job and bills and schedules and you get the picture. I was living the life of a responsible adult. My days were spent filling lunch boxes, sorting socks, attending ball games, and managing the never-ending mound of responsibilities that drain the energy out of every young family.

And then, I blinked! You may have experienced a "blink" yourself—that proverbial flicker of time, which spans two or three decades in a matter of seconds. One moment you're holding a little child who stares back at you in wide-eyed wonder, and the next you're clearing their bedroom after they've left home to spread *their* wings.

Sitting in that lonely room, boxing up my youngest child's high school memorabilia and fighting back the tears, I recalled the many years of our family adventures. I thought of my accomplishments thus far and pondered whether they had been a swing or a miss. Was I still on track for my life to account for anything as impactful as that of my grandparents? And was I finally *ancient*?

Here I stood at what should be considered one of the better places in life. The kids were grown, our careers were advancing, and we were living in a clean and quiet home. All of these were goals I had only dreamed about obtaining just years before. But it felt unreal, even hard to believe. I was now at the same stage as was previously unimaginable for me as a teenager. I had climbed halfway up the mountain of life, into the so-called "middle" years. And there was a definite hesitation to begin the ride down. But life moves fast.

To celebrate our fiftieth birthdays, my husband and I spent a vacation in Maui, Hawaii. At the center of this island is a massive and dormant volcano, topped with a beautiful national park called the Haleakala Crater. Early one morning we thought it might be fun to view the sunrise from the top of the crater, followed with a bike ride 6500 feet back *down* the mountain.

Just after dawn, our group had a quick lesson on how to use the specialized bicycles that would carry us down the slopes of Haleakala. We were handed a helmet and sent off to begin the 26-mile ride. The road contained several switchbacks that ran through Maui's upcountry and concluded at the beachside town of Paia. Bear in mind, the route followed along the literal edge of the mountain for almost the entire distance.

As we started out, it was invigorating to think of blazing down the mountain, with the wind at my face. Just picture it: An exhilarating bike excursion down the middle of a tropical island. Sounds quite romantic, doesn't it? But the actual ride turned out to be more *terrifying* than romantic!

Every time I came up to a switchback, there was the natural temptation to grab the handbrakes mounted to the bike. But using a brake while heading downhill at a high rate of speed posed the threat of my bike flipping end-over-end or worse yet, flying over the side of the mountain.

Our tour guide cautioned me from the window of the van tailing our group. "Mrs. Granberry, you can't use your brake when going downhill that fast. You'll have an accident. Just peddle on through the curves." *Easy for him to say; he was in the van!*

The steeper the slope, the more I braked. The sharper the curves, the more I braked. My bike fell farther and farther behind the rest of the riders, because I refused to peddle during a curve, but instead chose to slow down. It's a wonder I didn't go right on over that mountain. About halfway through, I pulled off to the side of the road and traveled the rest of the way down in the comfort and safety of the van.

I missed a very remarkable adventure that day because I didn't trust the advice of experts. My fear of heading swiftly downhill stole what should have been a great experience. My comfort zone shrunk to the size of my limited understanding of speed and incline.

Life moves fast. And you've got to peddle on through the curves. This is just one of the many powerful lessons I learned after reaching middle age. And throughout this book, we will explore the proper way to take that proverbial ride downhill.

Because if you're like me, or one of the other 80 million older adults in America, you may be wondering:

> *How do I make my life a story to be shared?*
> *What impact will I make on the world with the rest of my life?*
> *Will I choose to miss the thrill of a lifetime by dragging my feet as I continue to age? Or will I pedal on through the curves?*

Do any of these questions sound familiar? They may because these are the primary thoughts you feel after hitting midlife. They center around the realization that life moves along rapidly, and with that comes a hope that the remainder of your time counts for something! You seek a higher purpose and objective.

Little did I know that just a few years after my downhill bike ride, an encounter at age 56 would bring even *more* concerns about my God-given purpose, along with a few surprises about my relevance to the world. Read on to learn how I personally ended up in a box!

CHAPTER 2

WILL SOMEONE LET ME OUT OF HERE?

Rejection doesn't mean you aren't good enough; it means the other person failed to notice what you have to offer. MARK AMEND

IT WAS THE PRIME OF MY LIFE, fifty-six years old and living the dream. The time-consuming days of childrearing were a thing of the past, as my own children were grown and now busy parents themselves. While my elderly parents needed my support, it was manageable. I was wiser and more self-assured than ever, having survived the vanity of youth and the struggles of early adulthood.

My career had never been better. As a corporate director, I was traveling the world to manage teams. My resume featured exciting opportunities, like saving our company money by integrating new processes in less time than expected. I could corporate-speak with the best of my peers and felt relevant, essential, and grateful to use my talents in making a difference.

That is, until the wall—the brick wall. The proverbial wall that I slammed into mentally, emotionally, and somewhat physically. Perhaps you've hit that same wall along life's way. At one moment, time is rolling along in a consistent, predictable rhythm. And then out of nowhere, comes an event or circumstance that knocks you to your knees.

Looking back, I should have seen it coming. It must have been predictable because I was working sixty to seventy hours a week, going a hundred miles an hour and taking little or no care of myself. Business travel was at an all-time high. There were upcoming mergers, acquisitions, and implementations to oversee. And I wasn't about to stop.

My days were so jam-packed I would often wake up not remembering what time zone I was in or what day it was. The weekly routine included flying out on Monday, returning home on Friday, along with caring for parents on the weekend. Then, metaphorically rinse and repeat.

It was easy to ignore the fast tempo because life was thoroughly enjoyable. Hard work had paid off and big goals, made as far back as college, were now being attained. At my annual performance review, completed two weeks before hitting the notorious wall, I shared my desire to work "at least another ten years," to continue up the ranks. What was I thinking? Who can realistically sustain that kind of pace indefinitely?

The wall brought it all to a screeching halt and came in the form of a week-long hospitalization with a diagnosis pointing toward the silent killer known as *stress*. I had collapsed at my office while heading out the door to the airport, and now it was apparent that a drastic change was in order. This beast was utterly deteriorating my health. Without a life adjustment, I probably wouldn't be around much longer.

And so, I quit. I packed up my belongings and left that high rise office building in the rearview mirror. Completely out of character for me, I literally sat at the desk one day and then walked out the next, without even looking back. Throughout my career, if I made the decision to leave a job, it was because there was *another* purpose waiting ahead. But in this instance, there was no purpose that I could foresee—except the critical need to care for my tired self.

After a few days of rest and relaxation, I asked God where to head next. My personality doesn't relate to sitting still. I have to be accomplishing, contributing, or making things happen, always. And I knew the Lord wasn't through with my life, nor did I believe that nearly four decades in the workplace had come to a screeching halt. There was something else. But what?

At that time, we attended a moderately-sized church. Over the years, it had been a blessing to serve in various ministries within the congregation. The church staff consisted of gifted young adults who were still developing their ministry. We were close to the pastor, a talented preacher in his late thirties. Months earlier he had performed the vow renewal for our thirty-fifth wedding anniversary.

As is common in many young congregations, there were some *gaps* in communicating news to the church members. More than once we had arrived for services on Sunday morning only to learn that a significant church affair was scheduled for that very day! Obtaining church news was difficult for some because the calendar of events was only posted through social media. Now that works for the younger generations, but people my age are used to announcements on Sunday or to receive correspondence about church matters in the mail. Although I participated in social media, it wasn't our primary source of information.

It occurred that I could volunteer my time in the church's back office. Being there a few hours per week would help me stay "in-the-know" regarding scheduled activities. There was also a sincere desire to give of myself in a small way since my free time was now plentiful. So, I contacted the church office and scheduled an appointment with our pastor.

As we sat in his office, along with the associate minister, I informed them of my recent leave from a corporate career. Desiring to give of my time, of course, without pay, I hoped to assist in the back office or within another administrative area. The pastor listened as I described my previous work, which included reconciling million-dollar budgets and leading teams across several countries. My direct question to him was, *"Is there an area of ministry where my God-given talents would be a benefit in any way to your congregation or staff?"*

"Humm," he said. "I'm not sure if we have anything." He seemed distracted by every little thing around him and showed very little interest in the discussion. Not wanting to prolong the conversation any further, I thought, *"Oh well, his loss"* and politely thanked him, shook his hand, and headed for the door.

Just as I went to leave, he said, "Wait! You attend the first service, right?"

"Yes," I replied. My thoughts excitedly raced ahead with the possibility that the pastor might want me to analyze service attendance. *I'll compile the data, put some comprehensive flowcharts together, and then summarize it all on a PowerPoint to present to the elders. Oh, this is right up my alley*, I thought.

But my excitement sunk as he said, "Great! We need some older people like you to serve coffee at the first service. Are you interested?"

Excuse me? What did he ask? Was I hearing him correctly? Did the pastor just call me old?

In my mind, his voice switched to slow motion as he went on to explain, "Our leadership has been hoping that we could attract *older* people like you to the church. And if our guests see an *older* person like you serving coffee, then they'll know that *older* people attend here."

Yada. Yada. Yada. You get my drift. I was going to walk right out of there if the pastor used the word "older" one more time in describing me! Feeling a little shocked, I politely mentioned that I would "think about it" and quickly left his office.

While driving home that day, a colossal wave of rejection tried to overtake me. *You're a loser. No one needs you anymore. What a mistake you made leaving your career. Why did you think that someone might want your advice or help? You're old and irrelevant to the world.* My mind was literally flooded with negative, defeating thoughts.

Two of my God-given strengths are organization and administration. It had been a long time since someone had passed up an offer of help where those areas were concerned. But at that moment, my pastor, my friend, and a person who was then an essential part of my spiritual walk had simply dismissed me. Was he saying there was no other opportunity to share years of leadership and experience, except to serve coffee? For one thing, I didn't even drink coffee. And for another, I wasn't old!

Don't get me wrong. If the Lord wants me to serve coffee, I'll do it. But I really didn't sense God's voice in the pastor's request to be the token "older person" for our church. Our conversation had left me feeling disappointed and totally lost.

It was just two days later when an international marketing firm contacted me by phone. "We noticed that you do a lot of online shopping," the caller commented.

My first thought was, *"How do they know this?"* But they were right; I frequently shopped online while waiting around in airport lobbies. The excitement of my purchases accumulating at home was a nice reward after extensive travel.

The marketing firm representative went on to ask if I was interested in becoming a "secret shopper" who completes surveys about their online shopping experiences. The firm would provide a credit card, and I would periodically use it to buy preselected items at their expense. After receiving each delivery, I would schedule a return, then complete a series of questions about the order process.

Perfect, I thought. It would be a real win-win because I would earn a little spending money while providing useful feedback to the company. The representative mentioned there was a "provisional shopping exercise," but if that went well for all parties concerned, then I was hired.

After that trial item was ordered and returned, I filled out the survey with detailed answers regarding the entire procedure. The company soon informed me that they were "very pleased" with my thorough responses and their HR department would be reaching out to set me up in the system. The onboarding went smoothly as well, and soon, everything was signed, sealed, and ready to go.

"We will be sending you approximately three or four shopping requests per month," the HR lady stated. She also mentioned that the orders would increase in frequency at a later date if I could manage the volume.

A month went by, and I hadn't received a single shopping opportunity, so I contacted the customer service department to inquire. A courteous young agent answered, and by the sound of her accent, it was evident she was in a foreign country such as the Philippines.

"Can you check to see why I haven't received any shopping requests?" I asked and gave her my information.

"Let me see...yes, I find you here in the system. However, I see that your status is deactivated", she responded, her fingers clicking away on the keyboard.

"That must be a mistake. All my paperwork was completed a month ago, and I should now be active. Can you check on that?"

"Yes. I can confirm that you were entered just recently. And then our system automatically deactivated you a few days later," the agent replied.

"How does that happen?" I asked.

"There is usually a notation when the system deactivates someone. Let me see." She was typing softly in the background, searching for an answer. "Ah hah, yes, I found it. You checked the second-to-the-last box. Is that correct? I believe that's why you were deactivated," the agent informed.

"The second-to-the-last box?" *Oh, goodness, I must have misinterpreted a question on my hiring paperwork.* What had I inadvertently done?

"Yes, ma'am. You checked the second-to-the-last box for your age. Are you between the ages of 55 and 64?" the girl politely asked.

"Well, yes. But what does that have to do with anything?" I asked.

"Typically, our company doesn't collect data from anyone in those last two age bands. Their survey responses don't fit our needs and don't apply to what we're looking for. I'm sorry for the trouble but thank you for your time." Her pure honesty may have revealed more than her employer desired! And, before I could even *hint* at the marketing firm's involvement in age discrimination, she disconnected the call.

Here it came rushing into my mind once again, that now-familiar flood of rejection. I was experiencing yet another dismissal of my gifts and talents, which might have benefitted an organization.

Had I become Rip Van Winkle and slept through a whole season of life? Why was my age suddenly a bone of contention? What was this inconsistency I was experiencing? Being in a certain age bracket was beyond my control.

This all felt as though I was living in a paradox—the contradiction between finally possessing a little knowledge and experience, yet not having anywhere to use it.

CHAPTER 3

THE GREAT CONTRADICTION

The idea of living a long life appeals to everyone, but the idea of getting old doesn't appeal to anyone! ANDY ROONEY

LIVING LONGER AND HEALTHIER is one of man's most significant accomplishments over the last one hundred years. In the early 1900s, life expectancy was around 48 years for a man and 52 years for a woman. Thanks to improved health care and the eradication of many diseases, people can now expect to live much longer. For the first time in history, reaching age 50 means you most likely have half of your life still ahead of you. The fastest-growing age segment in America is age 85 and over, with the second-fastest being 100 and above. Longevity is a tremendous success story.

And we're not just living longer, we're living *better*. Older adults have opportunities that their descendants never had. The benefits of physical, financial, and mental well-being abound because of technology and increased fitness. People today can live positively and productively, well into their so-called "bonus" years.

But living longer can also pose contradictions. For example, when you reach your sixties, and you remain in the workplace, you are given the impression that you should really get out of the way for younger employees to take over. But at the same time, you get the message that as a senior citizen, you're a burden on your family or society if you quit work or start depending on others for assistance in any way.

It can feel conflicting when we don't think of ourselves as older, but people treat us as such. A man in his early sixties boarded a flight one day and selected a seat next to a young soldier, fresh out of basic training. The two men introduced themselves and struck up a conversation. The older gentleman said that during their visit, the soldier kept referring to him as "Sir." Every time he did so, the 60-year old looked around for his father! He never thought of himself as old enough to wear a title commonly reserved for our elders.

There's no question, aging has some inconsistencies. A youthful midlifer shared that she was carded to buy wine, sold a "senior discount" ticket at the movie and received her AARP card in the mail—all in the same week! Another lady became a grandmother for the first time at age 47. Now eight years later, people mistakenly refer to this lady's granddaughter as her *daughter*. Oh, the joys of life!

There's another paradox commonly observed around midlife. It's what I refer to as, "The Great Contradiction." Allow me to explain.

Researchers have long recognized the correlation between a person's current status and their satisfaction with life. Not surprisingly, people who are employed generally find their days more satisfying than those who are unemployed. People who have completed their education are typically more content than those still in school. Factors like employment, marital status, and other social conditions can play a role in our gratification at any given moment.

One might surmise that as a person advances in their career or completes the raising of their children, and so on, they should become increasingly happier. If that assumption is correct, when charting happiness (as compared to the progression of age) it would be viewed as a line continuously moving upward, from age 20 on (see Fig. 1). This premise is based on that fact that each new decade brings new opportunity, increased knowledge, and therefore growing satisfaction.

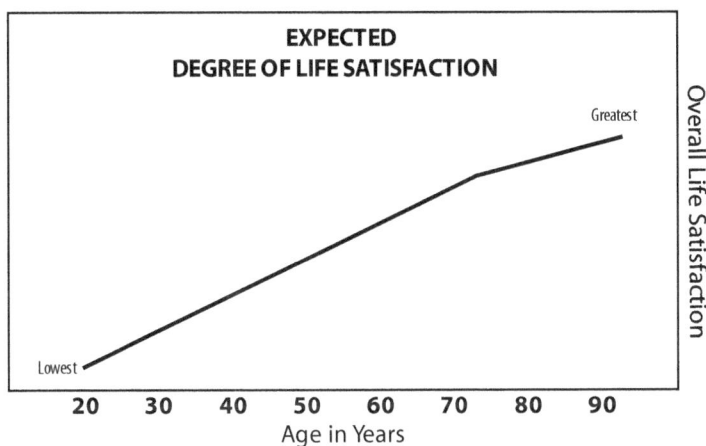

Fig. 1 Expected Degree of Life Satisfaction as You Age

But here are some surprising facts. After reviewing the results of a fifteen-year study on a person's happiness throughout each stage of life, award-winning journalist Jonathan Rauch wrote his book, *The Happiness Curve: Why Life Gets Better After Midlife.*

Take notice of one word in Rauch's book title: *Curve*. When charted in reality, a person's happiness graph follows a well-defined "U" shape, rather than a diagonal line (see Fig. 2). People in their twenties through forties usually feel a decrease in their life satisfaction, decade after decade. The lowest point hits at approximately age 50 before it begins to rise once again. And the research shows that this midlife happiness dip occurs to all people in every country, from coast to coast, whether you live on the plains of the United States or in the jungles of Africa.

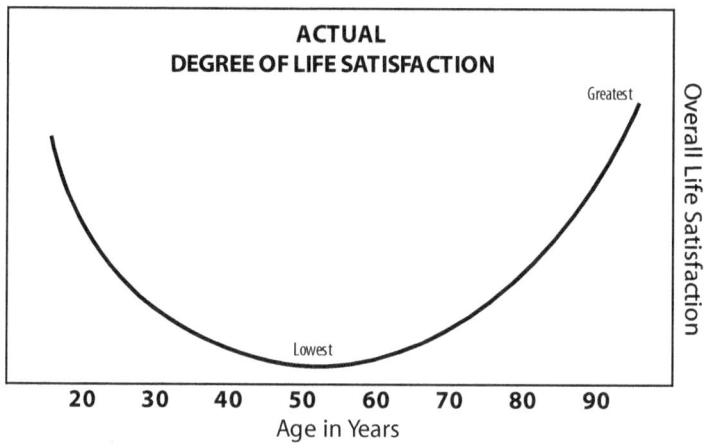

Fig. 2 Actual Degree of Life Satisfaction as You Age

At age 50, you are literally in the middle of something. You're the farthest from the proverbial edges on either side. In other words, you are no longer young. But you're not yet old.

Being in the middle isn't always fun and can feel like a slump! It brings a shocking realization of how much time has already passed. The distance between the busy days of youth is as far away on one side, as the time remaining before you enjoy the benefits of retirement on the other side.

Rauch doesn't attribute this happiness slump to a midlife crisis. He surmises that the downturn is simply a natural consequence—and an essential one. As you begin to shift your priorities and goals at middle age, your perspective also changes. You begin to fully understand what is vital and what is fleeting. And what you've done to find satisfaction at an earlier stage in life may no longer bring pleasure in midlife.

Social scientists believe that as people become older, they seek *true* happiness. Not happiness based on increased income, lofty achievements, or higher education, but through healthy relationships with family and friends, and from the joy in completing their life's purpose.

A few years ago, I directed a team of accountants staffed in Kolkata, India. It was my responsibility to make annual visits to conduct training and prepare for upcoming audits. Traveling to India takes hours and can be exhausting, so I would arrange to stay for at least 10 days each trip to minimize jet lag. My schedule provided time for tourism, as well. So, when visiting Kolkata one summer, a staff member had the great idea to visit Mother Teresa's home and grave.

Touring her residence was one of the most humbling experiences of my life. Mother Teresa had lived in a small room at the Missionaries of Charity clinic, which was an outreach she had established for people with leprosy. Her room contained only a twin bed, a dresser, and a small table which served as both a desk and a nightstand. Her space was void of any comfortable furnishings or the luxurious accessories that typically adorn a bedroom.

There was a worn Bible, along with a spiral notepad laying on the nightstand. The most unforgettable moment was when the tour guide pointed to a small stub of a pencil placed near the Bible, which had been sharpened down to less than one inch long. The guide explained that Mother Teresa was so prudent, she utilized every morsel of that writing tool to minimize unnecessary expenses and to focus on the critical financial needs of the mission. I also learned that rather than participating in the ceremonial banquet hosted for Nobel prize recipients, Mother Teresa had insisted the banquet funds were donated to the poor; the dinner would have cost nearly $200,000.

After returning home, I researched more about Mother Teresa and came across writings from her personal journals. I couldn't help but be struck by the words she shared. In the 1950s, somewhere near the *middle* of her life, Mother Teresa went through an inner "darkness" where she felt a battle raging.

During that period, she was wrestling with her faith in God at such a deep level, it brought pain and longing. She wrote about the "contradiction" within her soul:

> "Even deep down…there is nothing but emptiness and darkness…When I try to raise my thoughts to Heaven, there is such convicting emptiness that those very thoughts return like sharp knives which hurt my very soul."

How could the life of this dear woman be dark or empty? Her charitable work had impacted the lives of thousands, perhaps millions. She had made a promise to God at age 12 to love and care for the people that no one else would care for, and throughout the previous three decades, that vow had been honored.

Yet even Mother Teresa struggled with the paradoxes of middle age. While she publicly displayed strength in service to God, she privately had doubts and pain over her lack of total trust in Him. At the turning point of her career, she had reached the bottom ebb, questioning her call and purpose.

But the rest of her story is the best of her story. Mother Teresa went on to complete her most remarkable work—*after* hitting the lowest point of her existence. Over the next forty years, she used her incredible organizational and managerial skills to expand her Missionaries of Charity homes throughout the world. At the time of her death, over one million workers assisted her in 40 different countries. She was also honored with the Nobel Peace Prize.

During the second half of her life, she received numerous awards and accolades from popes, kings, and presidents. Even with deteriorating health, she continued her work until well into her eighties.

What Mother Teresa felt in midlife is often a common scenario. As young adults, we set high expectations that are often unrealistic. We overestimate who we are and what we will achieve. But as we grow in years, our view becomes less idealistic, and we begin to prioritize our goals more sensibly. Our gaze shifts from foolish optimism to profound hope in God. Viewing life from the middle causes us to reflect back over time and to move forward in faith as we trust God more with each day.

If you are right in the middle of your journey, begin to envision this time as the beginning of an *upward turn* in the happiness curve. Understand that this slump is a natural part of growth and that your very best days are still ahead. The fact is, all of us go through valleys—including the valley of midlife. But picture it like this: Valleys are positioned at the base of the mountains. And moving out of the valley takes you higher and to a new destiny.

If you are burdened with the emptiness and dissatisfaction of middle age, look to Mother Teresa's life as an example of turning the corner on the great contradiction that growing older brings.

CHAPTER 4

WHAT THE RESEARCH SAYS ABOUT BOXES

Some people will only love you as long as you fit in their box. Don't be afraid to disappoint.

THERE WERE SO MANY reasonable objections that came to mind after the marketing firm rejected me. Ideas that refute their presumption that the opinions of people 55 and over are irrelevant to consumer advertising. More than once, I contemplated calling the firm back to share my thoughts and give them a piece of my mind!

For example, at the time they hired me (age 56), I had more expendable income than ever before. And, I made informed decisions when purchasing big-ticket items, because wisdom and experience gained over the years had steered me toward quality and product excellence.

And what about the age bands that their employment questionnaire used to segregate applicants? The boxes were separated out like most surveys, dividing adults into groups for every 10 years from age 25 until age 65 (see Fig. 1). In other words, anyone 55 years of age would fall into the second-to-the-last box.

But it's that *last* box which really caught my attention. It appears to be a catchall for every person who is 65 and over. Does that mean my father-in-law, who is nearly 90 years old, makes the same purchasing decisions as a 70-year-old? Probably not!

AGE
18-24
25-34
35-44
45-54
55-64
65+

Fig. 1 Common Survey Age Bands

Understandably, the last band presumes most people who are 65 and over are now on fixed incomes, following a retirement. Most retirees fall into that last category. But my instincts tell me that not everyone in that group *thinks* alike, *lives* on an identical income level, nor *spends* the same. Even though members of this group have ages covering nearly four decades, they all get lumped together in a tidy little box called "65+."

Rather than discuss my opposition with the staff of the marketing firm, I determined to confirm my hunches with solid research. And then I would present the findings to a more global audience. You are in that audience, as you read this book!

What did I find after examining a group of people with opinions that are being passed over or put on the proverbial shelf? As it relates to spending in particular, here are some interesting facts. People aged 55 and over:

- Are more racially and ethnically diverse than any previous generation. *Talk about an excellent cross-section for a survey!*
- Use the internet more than any other age demographic, surfing online for around 11 hours per week.
- Rank shopping as the 4th most popular online activity spending around $7 billion per year.
  NOTE: Viewing the news, social media, and research take their top three spots for online use.
- Are poised to inherit almost $15 trillion by 2030.
- Control 70% of the disposable income ($2.4 trillion).
- Are responsible for approximately 80% of all luxury travel.

Will you please explain to me: Why are the opinions of this specific demographic not considered valuable? The people of the second-to-the-last-box have much going for them, and that should be a plus!

Wait—I just had an inspirational thought. Speaking of a group being a *plus*, perhaps that + sign used on the 65$^+$ label for the last age band actually signifies the *importance* of every person contained in it. This isn't a catchall box. It's one featuring people who are of tremendous value to society—they're a plus. Maybe that's it. Just a thought…let's continue on.

One reason we place outdated stereotypes on older people is that we really don't know who they are. We have negative predispositions based on the past and fail to see the benefits in their wisdom and experience. For instance, companies tend to believe that as a person ages, they will become more expensive to retain through increased salaries and higher insurance costs. But there is research which proves age is no longer a factor in the retention of good workers.

In fact, worker productivity tends to *increase* with age. A study from the University of Michigan showed that as the average age of a workforce increases, the overall productivity of the workforce rises proportionately. And people 50 and older tend to be more resourceful than younger, less experienced workers.

One crucial detail that no one can deny going forward is this: The landscape of our society is changing. As Baby Boomers continue to age, our population's average age continues to increase.

According to the U.S. census within the next decade, there will be *more* people over the age of sixty than those under the age of twenty. This is historical! As you can see in Figures 2 & 3, nearly twenty years ago the population trend was a gradual slope downward, as age progressed; however, the pattern for the next ten years is a gradual slope upward (the exact inverse).

Economists call this the "Graying of America." Sociologists refer to it as the "Silver Tsunami." Journalists mention the upcoming "Boomer Boom." Whatever the name for this phenomenon, the projected increase in older Americans is a fact that can't be denied. We should embrace the inevitable with positivity. We are living longer. We are healthier. There is a wealth of life experiences to share, and we are still useful to the kingdom of God. That's good news!

In Psalms 71:9, David wrote, "Do not cast me away when I am old; do not forsake me when my strength is gone." This statement echoes what I have felt personally in recent years. Have negative attitudes toward seniors been around longer than we think? I doubt that they used age bands to segregate people back in his day, but David was certainly feeling neglected when he wrote this passage.

Feelings of irrelevancy should not be a consideration as we grow older. Job 32:7 says, "Age should speak; advanced years should teach wisdom." Rather than putting people in boxes because of their age, maybe it's time for society to take the lids off and unpack the gifts inside. The research is straight-forward: People in the last two age bands have knowledge, experience, and wisdom to be shared amongst the generations. Let's open these boxes and share it!

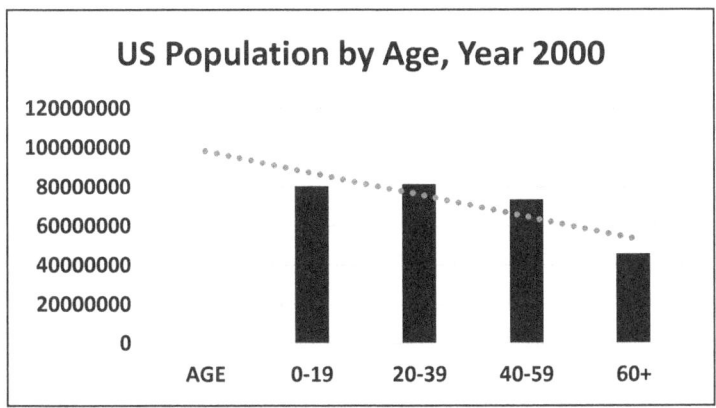

Fig. 2 – U.S. Population by Age in the Year 2000

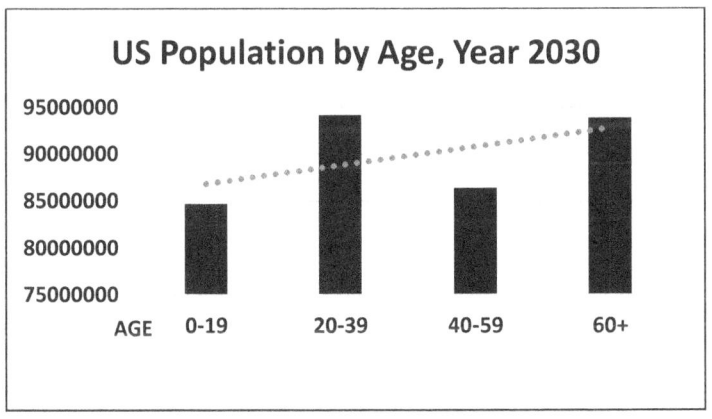

Fig. 3 – U.S. Population by Age in the Year 2030 (Projected)

CHAPTER 5

MIDDLE AGE OR MIDDLE MALAISE

You know you're getting old when your childhood toys are now antiques and collectibles!

BEFORE WE MOVE ON, I found this silly quiz online that you can review. It lists a few signs of middle age, or as certain people refer to it, "Middle Malaise."

It's true! After age 55, people start talking about their ailments and medical needs. They become painfully aware (*pun intended*) of the changes in their physicality and begin to display changes in their behavior, too. These changes are significant indicators that old age is rapidly approaching.

Don't take these personally—the quiz isn't meant to add insult to injury by belittling those of us in midlife. Quite the contrary, it should bring a smile as you embrace the reality that you're no spring chicken.

Review the list to see how many of these apply to you:

- Losing touch with everyday technology, e.g., phones, tablets & TVs
- Having no idea what those "young people" are talking about
- Feeling stiff
- Needing an afternoon nap
- Groaning when you bend down
- Not remembering the name of any modern bands
- Talking a lot about your joints and ailments
- Hating noisy places
- Getting hair-in the ears, eyebrows, nose, face, etc.
- Thinking policemen, teachers and doctors look really young
- Preferring a "night in" with a board game, rather than a night out on the town
- Not knowing any of the songs in the current Top Ten
- Choosing clothes and shoes for comfort, rather than style
- Obsessing over your garden or bird feeder
- Forgetting people's names
- Booking a vacation to a place that is "kid-free"
- Misplacing your glasses, bag, car keys, etc. (And often finding them on your person)
- Complaining that television "isn't what it used to be"
- Carrying tissues in your purse
- Seeing a friend from the past and thinking they look "old"
- Feeling the right to tell people exactly what you think, even if it isn't polite

If you could relate to over ten of these, it is time to accept that you are growing old.

If you could relate to *all* of these, you're not just growing old, you *are* old! But remember, God has a special place in His kingdom, just for you.

PART TWO

GENERATIONAL MINDSETS

CHAPTER 6

LABELS WE PLACE ON PEOPLE

Blessed be the tie that binds our hearts in Christian love; the fellowship of kindred minds is like to that above. JOHN FAWCETT

DESPITE THE GROWTH in the average age of our population, the negative mindsets and ingrained stereotypes regarding older demographics fail to change. Rather than seeing this group as a wealth of knowledge and expertise, society tends to view them as a drain on the economy and as a people with outdated ideas and traditions which must be changed.

Let's take a moment to consider the words we use toward people of every phase. As a famous comedian once pointed out:

> We are "going on" age 5
> We are "going to be" age 16
> We "become" age 21
> We "turn" age 30

We are "pushing" age 40
We "reach" age 50
We "make it" to age 60
We "hit" age 70

Do you see the underlying pessimism presented in this progression? While this observation was intended to be comical, the harsh reality is that we no longer view old age as something to be achieved, but rather something to be conquered!

The Bible says, "Gray hair is a crown of splendor; it is attained in the way of righteousness." (Prov. 16:31) Did you know that the word "elderly" originated from the Middle English word "elder," which referred to a person of higher rank, or a chief ruler and influential superior? To finally become an elder meant that through wisdom, someone was considered a prominent leader amongst their ranks.

The word elderly has lost its meaning and evolved into a connotation of someone helpless and dependent on others for support. That is sad because the concept is so far from what it used to mean. Why don't we view persons of maturity as accomplished, significant, and full of knowledge to be gleaned?

Commercial advertising reinforces the notion that aging is a problem to overcome. Ads are geared to help reduce wrinkles, cover gray hair, and minimize the telltale signs of growing older. One lady spoke about the time her young granddaughter reached up and squeezed the skin on her neck. Then the little girl grabbed the loose flap of skin under her grandma's arm and mentioned that it was "squishy." In her most loving and helpful tone, the girl finally suggested that her grandma try some Gold Bond Lotion!

In the same vein, a teacher divulged that she's heard it all from students when it comes to *her* age. One student asked her if there were colors when she was a child. Another pupil asked how she avoided being stepped on by a tyrannosaurus rex as a little girl!

When the vigor and spirit of the body begin to deteriorate, let's not reduce the worth of a mature person. We must value the influence of those who have lived a generation or two longer than us – wrinkles and all.

> For the Lord sees not as man sees. Man looks on the outward appearance, but the Lord looks on the heart. 1 Samuel 16:7

Along those same lines, we must recognize the importance and creativity of youth. The passionate dreams of younger generations bring excitement and wonder to a world that might otherwise be stagnant. I read an interesting article about three traits that young people possess, which are otherwise lost in older adults.

1. Smiles! Youth always have something to smile about. Their heart is typically free from the sorrow and pain that comes with life's challenges. Happiness is easily reflected in a child's perspective.
2. Appreciation for the little things. Ever notice how fun a box and some bubble wrap is to a kid? Their young imaginations see the joy in the small and in the simple.
3. Optimistic views. Seeing the glass as half full is natural to a child. Everyone knows the story of the child placed in the room full of manure. He kept digging and digging through piles of horse droppings. When asked what he was doing, the boy excitedly replied, "With all of this manure, there has to be a pony in here somewhere!" People of all ages should be looking for the pony!

Maybe it's time to clear our minds of all preconceived notions about ages and stages. All of us, be it a twenty-, forty-, or sixty-year-old, are made in the image of God or as it is referred to in the Bible, *Imago Dei*. The term isn't referring to *bearing* God's likeness. It suggests we *are* God's likeness. Whether we have gray hair and wrinkles, or pigtails and freckles, we are the image of our ageless God.

Take this to heart: We don't *have* his image, like owning something. Back in Biblical times, the kings would have idols fashioned out of wood and stone to be the physical representation of their gods. However, the chosen nation of Israel wasn't allowed to create idols or images because God had already made images of Himself. God's image isn't something to be owned.

We *are* his image. We all share his characteristics. Now don't misunderstand. We aren't God. We are His *likeness*. What do we all have in common? The task of collectively reflecting the image of God. Do you want to know what God looks like? Look at all of mankind – young or old. All of us have His likeness.

God is for people of all ages because He *never* ages. Let me repeat that again—God never grows old. He is the same yesterday, today and tomorrow. Here's the best way to feel young. Fix your eyes on the one who is ageless, timeless, and who cares about every single day of your life, from the day of your birth until the day of your death.

The Lord will carry us like a lamb when we are young, and He will hold us up when we are too feeble to walk on our own. Isaiah 46:4 reads: "Even to your old age and gray hairs, I am He, I am He who will sustain you. I have made you, and I will carry you; I will sustain you, and I will rescue you," says the Lord.

And at the heart of God's image is the truth that every single person has inherent value. God is our example; we must determine not to define His people by their age, race, or social status. As a society, we must relate to others by who they are, not how old they are.

What if you didn't know how old you were? Would it make a difference in the way you acted? Well-known author Wayne Dyer was out running one day along with his wife. At the time, he was 55 years old. There was a fence ahead, and he took off running toward it, intending to jump over the railing. Just then, his wife shouted, "You can't do that!"

But too late, Wayne had flown over and cleared the fence. When his wife caught up to him, she said, "Wayne, you can't go jumping over fences like that. You're 55." To which he replied, "I forgot!"

Don't hold on to inflexible ideas about what you should or shouldn't be doing at a certain age. And rather than perpetuating false views and theories, remove the labels regarding people. In showing respect for all stages of life, you will be the best you can be, all along the way.

CHAPTER 7

WHAT'S IN THAT BOX?

Age is an issue of mind over matter. If you don't mind, it doesn't matter.

MARK TWAIN

ALL ADULTS LIVING TODAY were born into one of six different generations, spanning nearly 120 years. Each generation's persona stems from historical events and circumstances that occurred during their formative years, and members typically share similar ideals, values, and traits over their lifetime. The groups and their corresponding birth years are:

GENERATION:	BIRTH YEARS:
GI Generation	Born 1901 to 1926
Traditionalists (Silent)	Born 1927 to 1945
Baby Boomers	Born 1946 to 1964
Generation X	Born 1965 to 1979
Millennials (Gen Y)	Born 1980 to 1995
Generation Edge (Gen Z)	Born 1996 to 2010

Outlined below are the common traits and influences for each generation, including shopping habits, motivational preferences, and preferred style of communication. Bear in mind, these aren't hard and fast descriptions because not everyone responds in the same way. I've already stated that I oppose human boxes and labels. But I do appreciate the science of Sociology because there is merit in the theory that we are shaped in part by the unique events and nostalgia of the world during our childhood.

Three key trends shape generations: Parenting, Technology, and Economy. For example, the philosophy of Baby Boomer parents was, "We want our kids to have it better than we did." And now they have produced the Millennials, one of the most entitled generations alive.

As you will note, there are significant differences between the generations. Case in point: A college professor was explaining the phenomenon left in your eyes from a flashbulb camera; he was perplexed to see his students just sit there expressionless. Come to find out, they had absolutely no idea what a flashbulb camera was!

Preparing this list made me smile because I know people from *every* generation; they each respond differently to the world. And after researching and compiling this outline, I completely understand why! Remember my story at the beginning on preferences for obtaining church news? Some people want to read a newsletter rather than a social media post. It's a generational thing!

Once you review the unique conditions that have impacted each generation, I believe you'll have a better grasp of our differences. And I hope it will serve as a bridge in communication and enhance the day-to-day interactions between us.

GI Generation (born 1901 to 1926)
- Formative years were during both world wars and the Great Depression
- Have a strong sense of civic duty, including voting, and loyalty to church, schools and their former jobs
- Marriage is for life (in their day divorce or having children out of wedlock was not widely accepted)
- Raised in a time when there was no social security for their parents. People worked until they died or could work no longer.
- Grew up without modern conveniences like television, air conditioning, refrigerators
- Lived with fixed standards of right, wrong and personal morality

Traditionalists (born 1927 to 1945)
- The Big Band and Swing music generation
- Formative years were during World War II, the Korean War, and the atomic bomb
- Women primarily stayed home to raise children; if they worked outside of the home, it was in stereotypical jobs like teacher, nurse or secretary
- Avid readers, especially the newspaper
- Gathered around the radio for family entertainment
- Lived to work; most pledged loyalty to their employer and kept their same position for life
- Self-sacrificing and disciplined
- Worst offenses in school were chewing gum and passing notes
- Retirement was the brief time after leaving work where you lived your final days

Baby Boomers (born 1946 to 1964)
- This generation started after the end of World War II; most Boomers were conceived after soldiers returned home from the war
- Formative years were during the Vietnam War
- The "me" generation
- The Rock and Roll music generation
- Started buying big-ticket items on credit
- Women began working outside the home in vast numbers, thereby creating two-income households (and women began working in jobs previously held only by men)
- The first generation to watch TV for entertainment
- The first generation to embrace divorce as acceptable
- Retirement became something to look forward to, as a "reward" following years of hard work
- Driven and optimistic
- The Beatles, the first moon landing, birth control pills, the John F. Kennedy assassination, civil rights

Generation Xers (born 1965 to 1979)
- With more woman working outside the home, their children became "Latch-Key Kids"
- Have hopes to save their own neighborhood, but not the world

- Feel overlooked by two of the significant generations (Baby Boomers and Millennials); often referred to as the "Sandwich" generation
- MTV, Atari, AIDS, the Simpsons, Ronald Reagan era
- The first generation to use of personal computers in their home
- Space Shuttle Challenger disaster
- They like to change jobs frequently, averaging seven career changes over their lifetime
- Very into brand names and designer clothing
- Self-absorbed and suspicious
- Have a lot of credit card debt
- Typical school problems involved drug use

Millennials (born 1980 to 1995)
- Formative years during 9/11, and the Iraq and Afghanistan wars
- Schools terrorized following the Columbine shootings
- Tattoos, body piercings
- The Internet, Chatrooms, Facebook, and Twitter
- Smartphones
- Reality TV became a favorite form of entertainment
- Over-schedulers
- Enormous academic pressure and high expectations for themselves
- Need constant recognition and to be told that they are special
- Work to live rather than live to work

- The first generation to grow up in a digital environment with unlimited access to information
- Like to collaborate in their jobs and work in teams

Generation Edgers (born 1996 to 2010)
- The first generation to have their own cell phone during formative years
- Have never known a world without computers or cell phones
- Are burnt out by the "ecological" talk and don't care as much about saving the environment
- Their children are playing less with toys and more with electronics
- Same-sex marriages
- YouTube, WIFI, Netflix, Barack Obama, ISIS, Snapchat, Minecraft
- Oversaturation with brand names
- Want participation awards
- Use cry rooms when they feel anxious
- Self-taught through online learning
- Access to "On-Demand" entertainment; no need to wait until the DVD comes out like their parents had to
- Last generation living with a Caucasian majority in the US
- Best savers (65% have a college savings plan)
- Sandy Hook shootings, the Boston Marathon bombing, Orlando nightclub shooting

This summary barely scratches the surface on the diversity of beliefs and experiences for people born within various periods. If you want to learn more, there are numerous books written to address the sociological science of the generations.

Let me point out two things that all generations have in common. First, every person has lived through significant historical events. Be it the Vietnam War or 9/11, a school shooting or an assassination, each of us has been shaped by the world around us.

Secondly, change has occurred and will continue to transpire. Our favorite forms of entertainment have changed. Technology has evolved. Our home and school environments have morphed into something entirely diverse from those of 100 years ago. Wars have ended, and others have begun. Jesus teaches in Matthew 24 that there will *always* be wars and rumors of wars until He returns to establish peace once again. All future generations will encounter influential world events during *their* formative years.

Here's the takeaway, our mutual ground is Jesus. The Bible says, "Jesus Christ is the same yesterday, today and forever." (Heb. 13:8) When the world seems unstable or ever-changing, God is unchangeable. His throne is forever, and his years will not come to an end. He has walked with every generation since the beginning. In the book of Daniel, we are taught that His kingdom is everlasting, and his dominion endures from age to age.

We must ensure that every generation teaches the next about God's truth. Psalm 145:4 says, "One generation shall praise Your works to another." Young people may never comprehend what an eight-track tape is or appreciate how a flashbulb camera worked. But they must always know that God loves them and is for them.

Do you know the biblical story of Esther? She was a Jew living in exile who actually rose to become the Queen of Persia. Esther's parents died when she was a child, and she was adopted by her Uncle Mordecai, a noble of the Persian King Ahasuerus. King Ahasuerus had a wife named Vashti, who fell into discord with him. So, he ordered all maidens to be brought before him to select another wife.

Esther, who was only fourteen at the time, was remarkably beautiful and the king was immediately taken with her. He made Esther his new queen. Her Uncle Mordecai continued to work near the palace and would consult Esther in stately matters from time to time.

One day Mordecai overheard a plot by eunuchs to overtake and kill their king. He told Esther, who then told King Ahasuerus. This foiled plot helped both Mordecai and Esther earn the king's trust.

Later Esther was able to save her people from a massacre. The prime minister of Persia issued a royal decree calling for the slaughter of all the Jewish people living within the Persian Empire and for the confiscation of their property. The prime minister hated Mordecai, and this was an act of revenge against him.

But Esther, being Jewish herself, risked her own life and after three days of prayer and fasting, she skillfully orchestrated the opportunity for her people to defend themselves and be saved.

Esther's life had been tragic during her formative years. As a child, she never expected to lose her parents or to be sent to live with a relative. She never foresaw the oppression that would come upon her people or the part she would play in facing the enemy straight out.

But God had his hand on her life. After the decree was issued to kill her people, Mordecai encouraged Esther to talk with the king. Her uncle told her, "Who knows if perhaps you were made queen for just such a time as this?"

God had ordained Esther to be born in the right place at the right time, to save His chosen people.

God didn't limit her because of her age, stage, or past. He didn't think, "Goodness, she's so young. She hasn't been around long enough to accomplish this." He could see the possibility in her to make a difference at that given moment. As a young woman, Esther had chosen the role of service rather than serve us. And God honored her prayer and fasting and gave her a life-saving opportunity.

What if you know someone who is an "Esther" today? What if there is someone from a generation other than yours who was born at the right time and the right place to save a nation? Will you limit them from becoming all that the Lord has planned because you have a differing opinion or feel that they are too young?

And most importantly, just like Esther, God has placed you and me right where we are and at this particular time in history. We were born for today, for this very moment. He has assignments for us that are invaluable to His kingdom.

I pray the Lord will help us break down the barriers created from the world of our past. Join me in asking God: *Please guide me to live out the role You have chosen for me, in such a time as this. Thank you that I was born at this time and was given this moment for You to accomplish Your purpose both within and through me. Amen.*

CHAPTER 8

WHAT WE EACH HAVE AND WHAT WE ALL NEED

Fear of the Lord is the beginning of knowledge, but fools despise wisdom and experience.
PROVERBS 1:7

A PERSON'S SUCCESS in life is shaped by three distinct areas: knowledge, experience, and wisdom. These concepts may seem similar, and you may have used the words interchangeably. But they are very different.

Knowledge is the accumulation of facts and data. Experience is living out the application of those facts and data. Wisdom is the ability to judge which of the facts and data are most applicable to your life. Someone cleverly described it like this:

Knowledge is about having the right answers.
Experience is about asking the right questions.
Wisdom knows which questions are worth answering.

Throughout this section, we will explore each subject thoroughly to better understand how they guide our decision-making. First, let's look at knowledge.

With information readily at our disposal, society is more empowered with knowledge than ever before. Google—Siri—Alexa—Wikipedia—the list of smart technologies goes on and on. You simply ask (or type) a question about any subject, and the answer pops up immediately.

The Millennial generation is the first to have had access to the Internet throughout the entire span of their formative years. To them, having a smartphone isn't just a modern convenience, it's a way of life connecting them to the world. They don't understand what it is like to rely on an encyclopedia or spend hours in the library researching for a term paper. Every bit of knowledge is right at their fingertips.

Your brain doesn't need to hold all the information, because your phone does! A few years back, my family was eating dinner together and chatting about former presidents. I couldn't remember who served before Richard Nixon. Within 30 seconds, my son pulled out his phone, googled the answer, and ended the discussion. A teacher told me that schools no longer require students to memorize the state capitals because if they "need to know them," they may easily search the internet for an answer.

And what about maps? Millennials have never had to rely on those big, clumsy posters to find their way around an unfamiliar area. They just plug in an address, and their navigation system tells them where to make a turn, along every step of the way.

Although it is convenient, utilizing technology to obtain knowledge is a mixed blessing. Not everything that's written on the Internet is accurate. The facts of science and history can easily be skewed into opinions when published online. People sometimes share their individual perception of a situation, rather than what is correct. Anecdotal information isn't always 100% truthful. People who rely solely on the so-called *facts* published online could be misinformed.

I have to wonder if the world wide web collapses one day, even for just a short period, what then? How will our Millennials get their information? The Internet has become the entire foundation of knowledge for a whole generation of people who depend on it to get around, to learn, to stay connected, and to collaborate with others.

As the saying goes, "Knowledge is power." And I'll give it to the younger generations. Knowledge is much more readily available than it was when I was growing up. So, if younger people hold the information in the palm of their hand (*literally!*) then in the game of life, they hold power. Ding ding. One point for them!

How about experience? Experience is gained over time. It comes when you've had extended contact with, or observation of, a process or event. Unlike knowledge, it can't be measured or tested in a quantifiable way. Experience is the growth that results after putting your knowledge into practice.

After graduation, I was trained in Accounting, but I had no prior involvement in that field. It required working as an accountant over many years to gain experience. I'll never forget my first time to participate in a state audit. I remember thinking, *I have no idea what they are going to be looking for or what to expect in this process*. But after a few years of involvement in annual audits, my experience grew, and there were fewer and fewer unknowns.

It was the same when raising our children. When we brought our first child home from the hospital, we were absolutely green behind the ears! Sure, we had read every book and attended a few informative classes. But we had no experience in parenting. I called my mom every time the baby made a noise or a gasp because it was all new to me.

Having some firsthand training in childrearing made it much easier when we brought our second child home. And ultimately, by the time we had raised both of our children safely into adulthood, we more fully understood their feelings, actions, and needs. Our parental experience came through long-term involvement in their upbringing.

Experience is a delicate combination of both success and failure. For example, as parents, we weren't perfect by any means. There were times when we made mistakes and had to ask our children for forgiveness (and each and every time we messed up, we would thank the Lord that tomorrow was another day to try again). Despite our flaws, we kept pressing forward.

You see, experience comes through action and participation. The origin of the word is the Latin *experientia* meaning "to try." One of my favorite quotes is from Oscar Wilde, who said, "Experience is one thing you can't get for nothing!" Merely reading a book on how to raise a child wasn't enough. We had to get in there and do it.

Your memory is built through experience because that is when information becomes a reality. As mentioned previously, when I first started in Accounting, I didn't know what to expect during audits. With every examination, my brain logged new details about actual situations that arose during the process and stored that information in my memory. Going forward, I recalled those memories, which in turn helped me better prepare for the next audit. Over time, my mind contained a wealth of information related to successful exams, and all obtained through my experiences.

James 1:22-25 (NIV) explains what happens when a person fails to rely on their memory (or experience).

> Do not merely listen to the word, and so deceive yourselves. Do what it says. Anyone who listens to the word but does not do what it says is like someone who looks at his face in a mirror and, after looking at himself, goes away and immediately forgets what he looks like. But whoever looks intently into the perfect law that gives freedom and continues in it—not forgetting what they have heard but doing it—they will be blessed in what they do.

When our memory retains what is learned through experience, be it something good or bad, the Bible says we are "blessed" in what we do.

Experience also takes time. That's one thing Millennials *don't* have on Baby Boomers—time in the game. While they may possess all the information, most have not lived through or participated in as many of life's teachable moments as the older generations. They haven't encountered every possible outcome that a situation might bring. Julius Caesar said," Experience is the teacher of all things."

When it comes to experience, time is actually on *our* side. Ding ding. One point for us!

Now to my favorite of the three concepts—wisdom. Wisdom doesn't arrive on your doorstep once you reach a certain age. It comes at the perfect intersection of both knowledge and experience. When a person is truly wise, they rely on both their understanding of the subject and the lessons learned through their practice of that subject, to make the best decisions possible. Referring back to the point I made at the beginning of this section, wisdom knows which questions are worth answering. A wise parent knows when to call the doctor and when not to. They combine their knowledge of signs and symptoms, along with their prior experience in gasps and gulps, to understand how to proceed.

Albert Einstein said, "Any fool can know. The point is to understand." We have a distant relative who's as "book smart" as one can get. Her IQ is higher than average. She learns knowledge and processes information quickly. When she has a choice to make, she'll spend hours researching all aspects of the matter to address her questions.

However, I would consider her *too* smart for her own good. Over the years, she has failed to learn from the memory of her experiences and has instead relied solely on her intelligence. And so, she makes unwise decisions, time and time again. Wisdom is gained through learning, but also through the failures and successes of your life, i.e., through your experiences. A person needs *both* to be considered wise.

Wisdom isn't dependent on age. You aren't handed a plate of in-depth understanding on your fiftieth birthday. I have known people who were well into midlife, with plenty of experience, but never coupled that with their intellect to become wise. And conversely, I have known young people, who used their limited expertise in a subject, along with information to make some very wise choices.

Solomon reigned as king over Israel almost three thousand years ago. As the son of King David, he accomplished his father's lifelong dream of building a temple in Jerusalem. In Jewish tradition Solomon is credited as the author of Ecclesiastes, Song of Solomon (insightful books contained in the Old Testament) and as the writer of many collections within Proverbs.

Scholars often refer to Solomon as the wisest man who ever lived. And, he was also one of the most foolish.

Although the Lord had gifted him with unparalleled wisdom, this king often wasted that wisdom by disobeying God's commands. Though he had all knowledge of God and His laws, there were times when Solomon failed to apply that knowledge to his own life; in those instances, he was unwise.

The Bible described situations when Solomon compromised doing what he knew to be right in the eye of God because it was a "small concern." He reasoned that these minor concessions wouldn't weaken his character; yet over time, they lead him into a significant life of sin.

In Deuteronomy 17:14-20, God gave Solomon explicit instructions against multiplying horses, multiplying wives, and multiplying money, where it is written:

> [The king] must not acquire great numbers of horses for himself or make the people return to Egypt to get more of them, for the Lord has told you, 'You are not to go back that way again.' He must not take many wives, or his heart will be led astray. He must not accumulate large amounts of silver and gold.

God had formerly delivered the Israelites out of Egypt. In essence, the Lord was telling Solomon, "I don't want you to go back to that experience again!" Solomon fully understood God's law and knew it would be wrong to import horses from Egypt or take additional wives. He had the knowledge, but he didn't obey God.

Throughout his reign as king, Solomon would violate one of these laws in a small way every so often. Just a little here and there. One wife, one horse, a little silver, a little more gold. And with each move, it drew him farther back into the bondage his people had been set free from, hundreds of years before. This brilliant man had learned nothing from the prior experience of his heritage. In failing to remember what God had done for him and for his people, Solomon moved farther away from God.

What words did Jesus give to his disciples as they sat breaking bread at the Last Supper? He told them to continue to "do this in *remembrance* of me." The disciples had witnessed incredible healings and miracles throughout their walk with Jesus. Those experiences were likely etched in their memory. But all of us tend to forget. And forgetfulness is dangerous because, like Solomon, it moves us away from the Lord.

Now Solomon probably thought, "It's not hurting anything. There hasn't been an earth-shattering result from doing things *my* way instead of God's every once in a while." In his case, God's wrath didn't come immediately following a violation of His laws, so Solomon thought he was getting away with it. In Ecclesiastes 8:11, Solomon wrote, "When the sentence for a crime is not quickly carried out, people's heart are filled with schemes to do wrong."

Solomon eventually became a fool who despised wisdom. He gradually drifted away from God, and when he grew old, he turned his heart from the Lord. Sadly, at the end of his life, he had become involved in pagan rituals and had committed the sins of idolatry and murder.

How does this pertain to midlife? All too often, we unwisely become stuck in the power of our knowledge *or* the value of our experience, rather than gaining insight from both. Becoming wise is finding the sweet spot between what we know and what we have lived. People in their middle years have adequate life experiences and sufficient knowledge to walk in wisdom if they choose!

Years ago, I had a friend share the short prayer she offers to God each morning. Her simple daily request is, "Lord, make me smart!"

My friend isn't asking for brilliance. She isn't asking for the exceptional IQ of Albert Einstein. My friend is asking for wisdom. She wants God to give her discernment about everything she has experienced in her past and pair that with her knowledge of His Word so that she may walk confidently through each day.

Someone once said, "Wisdom seems to be rare among any age group." Like my friend, everyone—no matter their age, should ask the Lord for wisdom. Possessing knowledge is a blessing. Gaining experience is a blessing. But when you ask for wisdom, God will enlarge your perspective through reflection over your life.

Through the Holy Spirit, you'll recall the memories of your experiences (both the successes and failures) and blend that with knowledge for guidance on making the best decisions for the remainder of your life. You will live in the perfect balance of answering the right questions moving forward, and through His grace, ignore the issues that don't matter. That is true wisdom and is what we all need.

CHAPTER 9

SERVICE OR SERVE US

Recognize that every interaction you have is an opportunity to make a positive impact on others. SHEP HYKEN

I HATE TO ADMIT that I am old enough to remember the days when gas station attendants pumped fuel, washed windows, checked tire pressure and handled the transaction for payment, without the driver even stepping out of the car. Back then, those establishments were called "service" stations, and that's exactly what you received, service.

Few would disagree that service, especially as related to pumping gas, has changed over the years. I recently tried to swipe my "frequent shopper" keycard while purchasing fuel at a local grocery store. But for some reason, the computer at the pump wouldn't accept my number.

So, I walked several yards to the counter where a young attendant behind the glass was busy playing on her phone. She was very perturbed that I had interrupted her. For a split-second, I thought, *Whoa, wait a minute. I shop here all of the time. I have more than earned this 10¢ per gallon discount! She should appreciate my business and be more helpful.*

But then it hit me—this young lady was at the stage where she knew nothing of *service* because she lived in the current world of "Serve Us." Like others at that period of life, her philosophy wasn't one of giving, but of getting. "I'll sit here and watch this booth for a few hours each evening, and my employer will give me a paycheck in return so that I can shop and buy things." That's the mantra of many young people.

It comes with the territory. Younger folks haven't yet reached the pivotal point in life where they feel a critical need to make a difference or to be a better influence on those around them. Their view of the world is based on another perspective.

I know you're thinking, *"Hey she's making a generalization! I thought she was against labels?"* Honestly, that's not my intention. It's not a label. It is a mindset for someone her age. Trust me, I was once young myself and viewed life with the same perspective as this young girl.

When you're young, it's about competition rather than contribution. As you start out in adulthood, you seek recognition. You work to impress people. It's about your accomplishments earned through competition. If you want to climb the proverbial corporate ladder, you've got to look better than the others or stand out in some way. You may have heard the joke about the old lady who said the "best" thing about turning 104 years old was that she no longer had "peer pressure!"

As we age, our focus changes. It's not about me. It's about others. And that change in perspective causes you to seek value by giving of yourself. You learn to work with others and contribute your gifts and talents to a team, to make a difference. You stand *out* by working *with* others.

Competition is a benefit in life because it helps you discover your capabilities and to strive to attain things you may never have believed possible. To a certain extent, competition makes you better. But when we compete only to obtain (i.e., to get something), we fail to learn a valuable lesson. You were created to serve (to give).

Do you recall the time when the twelve disciples got competitive? They had engaged in a heated discussion about who of them was the best. Let's look at what was recorded in Mark 9:33-36 (NKJV):

> Then He [Jesus] came to Capernaum. And when He was in the house, He asked them, "What was it you disputed among yourselves on the road?" But they kept silent, for on the road they had disputed among themselves who would be the greatest. And He sat down, called the twelve, and said to them, "If anyone desires to be first, he shall be last of all and servant of all."

The word "servant" comes from a root *servus,* which means "to minister." Service brings opportunities for ministry. Through ordinary tasks like assisting behind a counter, working at an office desk, or repairing a broken motor, you can demonstrate the *extra*-ordinary love of Jesus.

Roger Staubach, NFL Hall of Famer and former Dallas Cowboys quarterback said, "There are no traffic jams along the extra mile." Living a life of excellent service is often the road less taken because we view it as an inconvenience, instead of an opportunity.

Back to my gas station story: Rather than come home frustrated that day, instead I prayed for the young girl working at the counter. I believe she will come to understand that God has her in the right place at the right time to demonstrate His love. I trust that as she grows, He will lovingly change her heart from *serve us* to *service* and that she will recognize the opportunities God has given her to bless someone who is having a bad day or needs a simple smile.

Winston Churchill said, "We make a living by what we get. We make a life by what we give." The happiest people on earth are not those who are competing to be or to obtain the most. They are the people who have learned to make a life, by giving of themselves in service to others. And that is an excellent way to live—for all generations.

PART THREE

DO I REALLY BELONG IN THIS BOX?

CHAPTER 10

YOU AREN'T DONE UNTIL YOU'RE FINISHED

God is not finished with you yet. He is still putting your life in place just the way He planned it. Don't worry!

AS MENTIONED EARLIER, I don't care for the word "done," primarily when it's misused to refer to the completion of a person's God-given purpose in life. You may have heard the phrase, "Cakes are done. People are finished." Let's examine the origins of the words done and finished.

The dictionary defines the word "done" as no longer happening or no longer existing. It is the past tense of the word "do" and is synonymous with extinction, a thing of the past or being gone. When something is done, it is ancient history. Done is used when referring to one's behavior, relationships, or performance of an activity.

For example, a lousy marriage, ending in divorce, is done [no longer happening]. After becoming a parent, living wild and selfish days are done [ancient history]. You might ask a retired person what they *did* for a living, under the implication they no longer *do* that work—it is a thing of the past. But to believe someone's life is done when they retire is nearly disastrous! People are human *be*ings, not human *do*ings. And so, we don't cease to exist once we leave a situation that we used to "do."

The word "finished" means completed or concluded. It refers to the close or final component of an event or task. Finishing something is an accomplishment, as the word is more formal and absolute, expressing totality. When I finish my work, it means in its entirety, with nothing remaining. The word also implies that something has concluded well, as in a race.

As Apostle Paul approached the end of his life, he wrote in his second letter to Timothy, "I have *finished* the race, I have kept the faith. Henceforth, there is laid up for me the crown of righteousness, which the Lord, the righteous judge, will award on that Day." (2 Tim. 4: 7-8). Paul was handing the torch over to Timothy so that God's work would continue. But Paul, through perseverance to the end, had finished *his* ministry and completed it favorably.

In that same chapter, verse 10, Paul speaks of his coworker, Demas, who has deserted him and gone to Thessalonica. What do we know about Demas and why he left the ministry?

Demas is mentioned in other letters written by Paul as a fellow worker, along with Mark, Luke, and Aristarchus. Demas is described as a bright young man with a promising future. Even though he was a committed follower of Christ, in a short while, Demas deserted his ministry for love of the world. Paul and Demas had ministered together, but only one had finished. *Doing* the work of ministry was a thing of the past for Demas. But for Paul, living a life of ministry was completed thoroughly, totally, and worthy of a crown.

A multiple-choice question on the survey used to research this book was, *"I view retirement as..."*. The responses were:

- Just another season in my life's journey 65%
- A "reward" for many years of hard work 28%
- The finish line for a life well-lived 6%
- The end of what was a great road 2%

Less than ten percent of respondents chose an answer geared toward finality and conclusion. The majority seemed to embrace their post-retirement years as either another season in the overall totality of life or a time of reward following years of hard work.

Ending a career is not a reason to cease becoming all that we were called to be. History records numerous stories of people who achieved incredible accomplishments *after* they ended their fulltime profession. Some of these achievements came after a person's specific dreams had gone unattained, while others obtained victory after a challenging circumstance experienced late in life.

Have you heard of Colonel Harland Sanders? You have if you've enjoyed a delicious piece of Kentucky Fried Chicken. Rather than viewing retirement as the end of the road, it was only the beginning for him. At 65 years old, and shortly after receiving his first social security check, Colonel Sanders made a life-changing decision to take his famous recipe nationwide. He traveled the country, sometimes sleeping in the back of his car, selling franchise rights to restaurants.

It wasn't long before establishments all over America were frying up chicken cooked with those 11 secret herbs and spices. By age 73 the KFC corporation was sold for the equivalent of $16 million in today's dollars. Sanders never considered leaving his work in the restaurant industry; he remained active in the corporation until just one month before his death at age 90.

What about Astronaut John Glenn? If he had considered his work finished at age 65, he would have missed some great opportunities. Following his retirement from NASA, he served as a United States Senator for twenty-five years. While still serving in Congress, at the age of 77 he became the oldest person to travel in space, flying on the space shuttle, Discovery. Various experiments were conducted on this mission to test a 77-year old body in a weightless environment.

John Glenn was a man of religious devotion who served as an ordained elder in the Presbyterian Church. He believed that God was in him and often remarked that space travel had strengthened his faith. John Glenn lived a full and productive life until his death at age 95.

American baseball legend, Yogi Berra, is another example of consistently running the race. He was part of the team who had fallen far behind when participating in the 1973 National League pennant race. After the team rallied to win the division title, Berra coined the phrase, "*It ain't over until it's over.*" His famous words remind us to never give up because there is always an opportunity to finish well.

If you view retirement as just another season in life, you will continue the example of the Apostle Paul. You will stay the course and keep the faith until such time as the Lord completes your time on earth.

When you retire or make a change in your life after middle age, are you done? Or are you finished? It all depends on you!

CHAPTER 11

RETIRED? OR JUST PLAIN TIRED

If you get tired, learn to rest, not quit!

YEARS AGO, WHEN MY SON was a toddler, he would grow increasingly fussy just after lunch, and this would carry on well into the afternoon. I would try unsuccessfully to put him down for a nap, but he would kick and yell at me, demanding, "I'm not tired." Often, I would ask him, "Then why are you crying?" With a slight pause, he would always reply in exasperation, "Because I'm tired!"

Have you ever felt that way? Not wanting to give in because you knew it would be the agony of defeat. If you find yourself running back to the past as you age, you may simply be tired! You want to believe that your body still functions like it did years ago. But it won't.

I've noticed over the last decade that I don't work or move as fast as I used to. Years ago, my Saturday schedule included cleaning the house from end-to-end, running errands, cooking a couple of meals ahead for the following week and taking in a movie for entertainment. Today, it's impossible for me to complete even half of those tasks. *Sometimes I miss my former energetic self!*

The first step to solving any problem is to admit it. There are valid physical and mental reasons why our energy declines as we grow older. For example, aging muscles lose mass and strength. But there are simple strength-training exercises that can help you maintain flexibility and rebuild endurance.

And as we age, we need more rest. One study found that 50% of people over 55 in the U.S. have difficulty getting a good night's sleep. There are various reasons why, including restless leg syndrome, achy joints, heartburn, or just plain old worry.

A lack of sleep causes repercussive effects like memory problems, attention deficit, and daytime sleepiness. I've been in more than one board meeting where a middle-aged director nodded off during the discussion. Although it's understandable, sadly, it reflects poorly on the person and contributes to stereotypes.

Indeed, you should seek professional assistance if sleepiness is interrupting your day. And don't overlook the opportunity to ask God to help ease the problem, too. The Bible confirms that God wants His children to sleep well.

When I was younger, I didn't realize how much I wanted to be "in control" of every little thing going on around me 24/7. And I didn't understand that being a control freak was robbing valuable sleep. My parents came down to stay with us for one week, and while they were there, I felt so rested. It dawned on me that I had slept so much better during their visit.

I heard the Lord whisper to me, "You slept better because your father was in the house and you didn't have to be the one in control. But *I'm* your Heavenly Father and will watch over you every minute!" Right then and there I determined to put God at the helm each evening when I climbed into bed. It has made all the difference in my sleep. Give Him the worries of the day and ask Him to bless your rest with sweet peace.

Perhaps you need a vacation. We have friends in their middle age who are reluctant to take extended time off for fear that they will lose their job or appear to be disloyal. Remember that people of the Baby Boomer and Traditional generations grew up with a different attitude toward their employer; your worries may be unfounded.

Work is a gift from God. But He knows that in this fallen world, it can also be exhausting. That's why He commanded that we rest. It was part of God's plan from the beginning—to set aside time in our week for worship, recreation, and restoration. Thus, the Sabbath.

The root of the word "tired" ties to the word "weary" (Old English, *worian*) which means to crumble or break down. The Lord knows that you begin to crumble physically, mentally, and spiritually when you fail to take His commandment seriously. Being overly tired can often lead to weariness and ultimately to burnout and a state of exhaustion.

In Exodus, Chapter 18, you can read about a time when Moses worked every day, from morning until evening, resolving disputes amongst the people. He handled *all* of the cases himself, both the large and the small matters, and it was wearing him out!

One day Moses' father-in-law Jethro asked him, "What is this that you do for the people? You are not able to do it alone. This thing is too heavy for you." Jethro advised Moses to develop a plan to employ hundreds of able-bodied men, who feared God and would assist Moses in handling the small matters.

This made things easier for Moses and allowed him to rest. Jethro told Moses, "By doing this, God will direct you, you will be able to endure, and all of the people will go to their place in peace." It was a benefit for everyone.

Jesus said, "Come to me all you who are weary," and He would give you "rest." If you're at a point in your life where you see retirement as the only way to escape the pressure and worries of life, seek the Lord's guidance. Like Moses, if you're about to crumble under the strain of work, ask God for a way in a place where it seems there is no way.

Trust me—I've been there, done that. And I can say unequivocally that the Lord needs you to be your very best for this next season, and He *will* provide you with rest.

CHAPTER 12

ACT YOUR AGE

I don't like looking back. I'm always constantly looking forward. I'm not the one to sort of sit and cry over spilled milk. I'm too busy looking for the next cow.
GORDON RAMSEY

HAVE YOU ENCOUNTERED SOMEONE who always speaks in the past tense? "I used to be a teacher." "I worked at a company for XX years." Their lives seemed defined by what they were or what they did.

It reminds me of a theory floating around in recent years that suggests, "Sixty is the new forty." And that "fifty is the new thirty."

Are you curious about how this concept started? Did it originate with someone who didn't want to embrace the reality that they were growing in years? Perhaps it was the mantra of a person who needed more time to accomplish unattained goals set twenty years prior. The idea to be *fifty* years old, but to be perceived as *thirty*, sounds exciting in principle. But what about in practice?

The irony in making a comment like "sixty is the new forty" is this: You are still focused on the past, instead of the present. You are deceived into thinking that living like you're forty will buy extra time to fulfill your unmet dreams and expectations. God is not going to let one event from the past hold you back from the blessings He has for you ahead.

While there have been times that I longed for the proverbial clock to be rolled back, the truth is, that's unreasonable. Life marches forward. Every second, every minute, every hour moves us ahead. There's no turning back. The marvelous benefits of a particular stage in life cannot be a reason for us to stay there permanently.

Do I miss the fun and joy of a home filled with small children? Absolutely. Do I miss the rewards and benefits of launching my career? You bet. But physically and spiritually, I'm grateful for exactly where I am today! I don't worry about competition and proving myself. I'm comfortable with what I've learned and experienced in raising my children and throughout my career. Just like time, I'm moving forward.

Embracing your *current* age brings real peace of mind. If you focus on being forty, when you're *actually* sixty, then you'll miss the blessings that come with life at sixty. If you spend time and effort to return your physical appearance to that of a thirty-year-old (when you're really age fifty), you might become focused on preservation and not on vitality.

Mohammed Ali offered sage advice when he said, "People who see life in the same way at fifty, as they did at twenty are wasting thirty years of their lives." Living your life in the present moment is often a challenge. We tend to be caught in the past *or* overthink about what our future might bring.

Our lives are like cars, moving us forward through time. Cars have large windshields and relatively small rearview mirrors. You don't look back to the past but forge ahead to the future. Believing you're forty, when you're actually sixty, is similar to driving backward. The Word of God instructs us to "forget what lies behind and move forward to what lies ahead." (Phil. 3:13)

In reality, sixty is the *new* sixty. There used to be a time when that age meant your life was nearing a close—pretty much over and done with. As mentioned consistently throughout this book, that was *then*. Sixty is no longer the end of life; for many people, it's just the beginning.

Consider the following famous and influential people who had a successful second and even third act, after they were well into middle age:

Laura Ingalls Wilder was an American writer, best known for the Little House on the Prairie series of books. Beginning at age 16 in a one-room schoolhouse, Wilder taught children of all ages for most of her career. To satisfy her lingering passion for journalism, she wrote a few magazine articles over the years.

It wasn't until age 65 that she published her first novel, *Little House in the Big Woods*, which would eventually become a series and produce a hit television program. Wilder completed the last of her Little House books at age 76 and died at the age of 90.

If you enjoy baking cakes, then you've probably heard of Duncan Hines. At age 55, he compiled his first food guide, critiquing restaurants across America. His book was so popular, he included the review of hotels and lodging in his next handbook. Soon after, Hines became a food columnist featured in newspapers across the nation. It wasn't until age 73 that his delicious cake mixes were licensed to a food supplier and later expanded into national distribution.

The list goes on: Ray Croc, developer of the famous McDonald's fast-food restaurant franchise and Julia Child, well-admired cookbook author, both rose to popularity after age 50. There's another second-act lady you need to know—the fantastic Millie Garfield. At age 90, she is one of the oldest bloggers on the Internet. She routinely posts amusing stories of her everyday happenings, and people love her so much, they follow the blog just to keep up with Millie.

Everyone mentioned in this chapter is a person who wasn't bound up in the belief that they were done working or too old to start something new. And they didn't try to run back to a former time twenty years ago but instead embraced their current age with joy. They used their experience, skills, and even connections made over the years to steer forward, viewing through their windshield, to a better destination.

You might not be the next creator of a food franchise, but that doesn't mean you can't realize a lifelong dream. Write a blog, post a timesaving hack, or create a video demonstrating a "how to." Take your passion to the next level, to influence the lives of others.

What's the key to finding real purpose, later in life? A positive view of your future is essential. Rather than thinking, "I'm too old to start a business" or "People my age don't run triathlons," remove the limits you've mentally placed on yourself. Look ahead and realize that what is held in your future is higher than what was in your past. Have the confidence that you can still accomplish whatever you desire—because age is not a limitation.

Many have entered what is known as "The Third Chapter" following middle age. This is a stage where people are winding down lengthy careers and choosing to seek an encore performance. This curtain call is an opportunity to experience the liberty of doing what you *want* to do, rather than what you *have* to do. Believing that your life still makes a difference, you have the freedom to write your next act.

ACT YOUR AGE

At age fifty and sixty, you're at a different place than you were in your thirties and forties, and you're motivated by different things. The lens with which you view the world isn't clouded with idealism but with clear wisdom gained from three or four decades of experience. How many of us have thought, "I wish I had known then, what I know now?" Imagine if you were forty but had the understanding you now possess at sixty. Could life at your current age be of benefit to the younger people you assist or mentor?

Turning age sixty introduces a new season of life. Survey respondents confirmed this when choosing their favorite song about growing older. In Fig. 1 you can see the 1969 hit *"Turn, Turn, Turn—To Every Season"* (as sung by The Byrds) was the most widely chosen tune describing their life in the present. There *is* a purpose for the season you live in right now. Don't run back to the past and miss it, by pretending to be younger than you really are!

POSSIBLE ANSWERS	RESPONSES
Turn, Turn, Turn - To Every Season	29%
I Did It My Way	16%
Time Keeps on Slippin', Slippin' Into the Future	14%
Forever Young	12%
I Don't Need Your Rocking Chair	12%
Much Too Young to Feel This Darn Old	9%
The Old Gray Mare Just Ain't What She Used to Be	6%
Against the Wind	3%

Fig. 1 What Song Title Best Describes You

Acting your age brings a new point of view and a renewed outlook. Remove your glance from the rearview mirror of what life used to be. Focus on what lies ahead as you move into this next season of life!

CHAPTER 13

OUR BIGGEST CONCERNS FROM THE TOP OF THE HILL

I have enough money to live comfortably for the rest of my life…if I die next Thursday!

THERE'S NO DOUBT THAT, as we age, our needs change. Survey participants agreed on three pressing concerns, which consume their worries as they approach their golden years.

When asked, *"At my age, what are my biggest concerns?"* respondents overwhelmingly chose:

1) Not having enough money
2) Losing my mind
3) A decline in my physical health
(See Fig. 1)

POSSIBLE ANSWERS	RESPONSES
Losing my health	66%
The decline in my mental capacity	43%
Not being able to afford what is needed to live out the rest of my life	39%
Changes in my appearance	19%
Leaving a legacy for my family	18%
A younger generation changing the world from the way I know it	14%
Losing my job to someone younger and/or smarter than me	6%
Other	9%

Fig 1. At my age, what are my biggest concerns? (*choose as many as apply*)

I've summarized these fears into three simple words: Health, Wealth, and Self.

HEALTH:

From the day of our birth, up until the day we die, our mortal homes are decaying, or as the Bible refers to it "perishing." The word perish comes from two Latin roots: "ire" *to go* and "per" *through something completely*. Without sounding morbid, to perish means to die in a slow, gradual, nonviolent way. The truth is, our bodies are like clay pots that continue to wear away as time moves forward. However, the signs of wear and tear may not show up until later in life.

How many of us wish we had made better choices regarding our long-term health when we were younger? Some never realize that poor decisions made as young adults have resulted in devastating consequences years later. Healthy living won't prevent all issues, but most physicians agree that cardiovascular disease, adult-onset diabetes, and several other chronic illnesses don't just pop up overnight. They manifest after years of poor habits and even neglectful behavior.

Without getting on my soapbox, I hope that people of younger generations will come to understand the critical importance of caring for their physical self. Using a sunscreen, eating clean foods, and avoiding unhealthy vices are behaviors that will impact the length and quality of your life. Sowing seeds early will reap a harvest of good health decades later. *Perhaps this is an area that we, as older adults, can emphatically underscore to those we mentor!*

Our bodies can't be preserved. To preserve something means to keep it in its original or existing state. We don't have the body of a twenty-year-old when we are fifty. But we can, and should, work to *maintain* our health. To maintain something means to keep it in good condition or working order, by checking it regularly.

It's never too late to start. Positive changes made later in life have a favorable outcome on a person's health. For example, adding more fruits and vegetables to your diet lowers the risk of early death, as compared to people with poor eating habits. Just a 20% improvement in your diet reduces your risk of premature death by 17%. That is accomplished by substituting saturated fats for healthy fats and making other simple changes. Reducing sugars, sodium, and limiting the intake of processed foods also makes a difference.

Exercise is essential, too. You're never too old to begin a fitness routine. As we wind down, we become more sedentary. That's why it's vital to participate in a safe yet active workout program and to consistently stay with it. Movement and conditioning benefit your mind and spirit, as well. Studies show that staying active reduces the progression of brain disorders and delays the onset of dementia.

Science teaches that the determinants of good physical health are 20% genetic, 20% health care, and 60% everyday choices. Rather than being focused on the gradual decay of our bodies, we must concentrate daily on remaining healthy—physically and spiritually. 2 Corinthians 4:16 states, "Therefore, we do not lose heart. Though our outer bodies are dying [perishing], our spirits are being renewed every day."

The Lord created us with His own hand. He is fully aware of our needs before we even ask. Give the anxious thoughts regarding your health to God. Allow Him to fill your mind with ideas on how to restore and maintain. Honor God in every aspect of your life, including the physical care of your body.

WEALTH:

Life is expensive, and it doesn't get any cheaper as we age. Today, a majority of older persons worry less about leaving an inheritance to their family, and more about their resources lasting through the remainder of their own life.

According to AARP (formerly the American Association for Retired Persons), the number of persons age 65 and over who filed bankruptcy in 2018 has doubled since 1991. Part of the reason is the high cost of health care. Retirees have found that Medicare alone doesn't cover every need; the cost of copays, deductibles, and supplemental insurance has made it difficult for people on fixed incomes to make ends meet. By 2030, it is projected that Medicare will consume 50%

of a person's social security income. That leaves very little for remaining expenses!

Then consider that over half of all households living in retirement have absolutely no savings, and for those that do, their "nest egg" only amounts to slightly over $100,000. If invested at current rates, the return would provide an income of less than $500 a month. Only 14% of pre-retirees have accumulated the means necessary to support them comfortably during their later years.

Comedian Steve Martin once provided a humorous suggestion on how to get a million dollars and not pay taxes on it. It was a two-step approach. First, get a million dollars. Then, don't pay taxes on it.

Now if his silly advice were that easy to accomplish, we'd all be rolling in millions! But it never ceases to amaze me how many people put off financial planning until it's too late. Like the ridiculous counsel of a comedian, they carelessly live as if it will be a snap to obtain money when needed.

Statistics show that a 65-year old can expect to live at least another 20 years. Your savings must cover day-to-day expenses, medical costs, property taxes, and any unexpected needs that come up during that time.

The first step to financial security is to start early when saving for the future. Again, by following the spiritual principle of sowing and reaping, there will be a greater harvest financially when you sow seeds of saving as a young adult. Prepare for your ultimate transition *out* of the workforce, just as soon as you have entered into a new profession, by setting aside a portion of your earnings for retirement.

God's Word teaches us that even ants save a portion of their harvest for the future. Proverbs 6: 6-8 says, "Go to the ant, …observe her ways and be wise." These small creatures have an incredible vision, they are hardworking, and they know how to save for later. We are smart to walk in the same manner as the ant.

Perhaps you were unable to start saving for retirement before age 50. It's not too late. The law allows "catch up" contributions to IRAs and other retirement plans. Be determined to put more of your income into savings. Or consider working a few years beyond the traditional retirement age.

You won't get to where you need to be if you don't try. Ask the Lord to bless your efforts to increase your storehouse before retirement. Thank God for His supernatural favor. Believe that He will bring witty ideas to your mind so that you will have what is needed to live the rest of your life, free from financial worry.

The next step is to change your beliefs about money. Money is a tool to help you experience the best years of your life. Over the past few decades, you have exchanged your time for money, by working forty plus hours per week. Now use your time to focus on the resources you have and how to manage them wisely.

Find ways to save more and spend less. Reduce debts in advance of retirement. Do you have resources that may be sold or donated, to increase income or be used as a tax benefit? For example, a solution for some couples is to consolidate down to one vehicle. Determine to set reasonable expectations to live within your means and continually stay disciplined to walk in financial freedom.

SELF:

Have you ever caught yourself repeating something to a friend or relative? Have you experienced a memory lapse that caused you to forget your best friend's name?

A situation like this can stir panic within your mind because many people fear the debilitating effects of brain disease as they age.

Too many of us have lost a parent (or two) to the devasting grip of dementia or Alzheimer's. Even if you've been fortunate enough to have avoided that directly, you probably still understand the ripple effect that mental illness brings to friends and family.

Mental health comprises your psychological, emotional, and social well-being. Your moods, behavior, and ability to reason are significantly impacted when your mental health declines. Caring for your brain is as important as caring for your physical health. In fact, the two go hand-in-hand.

In the early 1900s a noted physician from Johns Hopkins, who was considered an expert in brain science at the time, delivered his farewell retirement speech. He mentioned that a person's brainpower and creativity had an expiration date. Unfortunately, his theory became widely accepted by other neurologists, who believed that brain cells died off without being replaced.

Thankfully, research today refutes this theory and links extended mental fitness to one essential element: Education. People who continue to learn from middle age and beyond delay their brain's aging process up to a decade. This isn't limited to higher education. It constitutes of a range of activities that improve our cognitive intelligence.

New research progresses on controlling dementia and Alzheimer's, although a complete cure has not yet been discovered. There are proven studies that identify the ability to maintain brain health through the following:

- Learning a new language
- Remaining socially active

- Learning something new
- Pursuing a new hobby
- Caring for a pet
- Playing games
- Working puzzles

Activity centers are popping up all over to provide physical and mental exercise for seniors. Many churches host events and classes for older adults. Explore opportunities in your area to join a club or organization structured for this.

And finally, shift gears, before you head down the hill.

Rather than focusing on decline and diminishment, focus on fitness and making daily choices that will benefit your well-being. HEALTH.

Rather than dreaming of being rich beyond your wildest dreams, seek guidance on having the financial means necessary to care for yourself until your death. WEALTH.

Rather than allowing age-related concerns to limit your participation in certain areas of life, seek opportunities in your church and community to maintain your physical and mental fitness. SELF

PART FOUR

WE ARE BREAKING OUT OF HERE

CHAPTER 14

LIVE IN THE NOW

Time is a curious thing. When you have it before you, it is something you take for granted and it moves slowly. Then, as you get older, it accelerates. BERNARD SUMNER

HAS IT EVER FELT that the forty hours spent in a week at the office seem to click by much slower than forty hours do when expended on a vacation? Why do six weeks of school seem to drag on forever, while six weeks of summer roll by in a flash? Does time really fly?

Time is a strange concept. There is no scientific evidence to prove that the seconds and minutes of one event move any faster than they do for another. And yet there are definite moments and situations where it seems entirely possible that time has *wings*. That is because our experience of time directly correlates to our attention, our motivation, and our emotions.

Psychologists explain that when we are young, we pay extraordinary attention to every little detail in the environment. (Notice I didn't say that a youngster pays attention to their parents or teachers. That's another discussion, for another time!)

Have you ever taken a short walk with a child? They stop to look at the sun and the sky and the ladybug and the butterfly and to touch the grass and to smell the flowers. They chase the bouncing frog and roll in the freshly cut grass. Children rarely miss a detail. And observing every little element around them causes the sensation that time is expanding. Time seems to move slowly for a child.

But as a person grows in age, they become much more familiar with their environment and tend to overlook the minute details surrounding them. Rarely does a middle-ager roll in the grass, chase a frog or even notice the insects in the air (unless they're fumigating their front porch)! Very few elements are *new* to an older adult, and that causes their time to compress or pass more quickly.

Being in an emotionally negative situation also causes our perception of time to move slow. Boredom, illness, depression, and anxiety are all factors which can stretch out time for individuals. These emotions drain our energy and rob our attention, making it seem like the days are even longer than usual.

Some people become "frozen in time" by dwelling on and speaking about life in the past. They say, "I used to be" or "I used to work at." This behavior is detrimental to your health and well-being and can cause missed opportunities in the present moment. God has new mercies for you every day; you miss today's blessing when you live in the past.

If you've been in a life-threatening situation, it probably seemed like time *noticeably* slowed down or even stood still. During a few treacherous seconds, your brain is processing an abundance of information and taking into consideration all possible outcomes. Because you record more of a traumatic experience in your mind, it extends time emotionally. Your concept of time is impacted by motivation, as well.

My husband, Sam, was best friends with a man named Virgil. As work colleagues, they had supported each other through the ups and downs of their respective careers for nearly twenty years. They made it a point to visit by phone daily, and the conversations often turned to their goals for life beyond the company. Virgil and his wife, Debbie, had plans to travel following their retirement, hoping to take long trips across America.

Since Virgil was a little older than us, we lived vicariously through him and Debbie—praying God's very best for their life, post-retirement. And, we looked forward to that day when we, too, could travel and experience a life free from the confines of our occupation and employment.

During that first year following Virgil's retirement, he and Debbie made considerable strides toward accomplishing their post-career goals. They built a beautiful home and purchased a truck and travel trailer to take on those extended vacations. It was amazing to see their plans unfold in such a short time. But they were motivated to make it happen.

I'll never forget the excitement in his voice as Virgil gave us a tour of their new travel rig. They would be leaving in just a few days, headed west for several weeks of exploration. There were no expectations of returning home at a specified time; after all, they were retired and would go as the wind blows.

Just days after leaving on their exciting adventure, and only one year to the day following his retirement, Virgil was killed in a tragic car accident. He and his wife had happily ventured out on their long-awaited trip, and sadly, their hopes and aspirations were cut short.

It was through Virgil's death that we came to understand life doesn't offer guarantees! My husband and I determined to live for today and stop putting things off for that elusive *one day,* which might never arrive. Benjamin Franklin said, "Don't put off until tomorrow what you can do today." Procrastination isn't the answer to accomplishing your dreams, particularly when you've turned the corner on midlife.

Since Virgil's passing Sam and I have made sincere efforts to remove words from our conversations that stall or defer; especially when it comes to making big plans and decisions. Instead of saying *"should," "might," "going to,"* and *"someday,"* you'll hear *"now," "soon,"* and *"today"* in our dialogue. That's all we have—today!

While we live on earth, we are bound to clocks and calendars and the movement of what is known as Chronos time. It is distinctly measurable as it marches each moment from the past to the present, and then into the future. Sixty seconds become a minute, sixty minutes become an hour, and so on. Chronos time can't be stopped, and it can't be reversed. One becomes painfully aware of the boundaries of Chronos time when they are given a prognosis, with a certain amount of time to live.

But think about this—what if you had a bank account and every morning $86,000 was deposited into your account? You had to spend every cent of those funds by the beginning of the next day. Nothing would be carried over from the previous day. You would be given complete freedom on how to spend that amount, but you had to draw out every cent, each day.

Well, that's how Chronos time works. Every day your life is credited with another 86,400 seconds. Nothing unused from the day before carries over to the next day. And there are no overdrafts; you cannot borrow time from tomorrow. Each day brings a fresh new deposit to your account.

In a way, Chronos is God's gift to mankind. It serves as a measurable resource that humbly reminds us of our earthly limitations. It hems us in. For example, in Matthew 6:34, we are instructed not to worry or be anxious about tomorrow. Our attention, emotions, and motivations do best when confined to the matters contained within 24 hours.

Now the Bible also refers to a concept called Kairos time. Kairos isn't about the movement of time but speaks to the urgency of the now. Living in Kairos time means turning our attention to God and away from the distractions of negative emotions or worldly motivations. When we choose to walk in Kairos time, we focus not on the quantity of time that remains, but on the quality.

Only God knows the exact number of years, days, and hours a person has left on this earth. Rather than being consumed with the measurable amount of time (Chronos) that remains for you, purpose in your heart to live every moment as if it were your last...or even your first!

Jesus taught that we must become "as little children." He understood that we can't reverse the clock and physically return to the days of our youth. Instead, becoming *as* a child means to be fully aware of the small and beautiful things that surround us.

Readjust your spiritual clock to live in the Kairos present time (after all, it is a gift, and that's why it's called the "present"). Each morning, thank the Lord for the privilege to receive His new mercies.

Ask yourself, "What am I going to do with these 24 hours called today?" View each day as the beginning of your life and make it count for something important. Trust your infinite, all-powerful, and all-knowing Father with the immeasurable *now* in your life.

CHAPTER 15

RETIRE TO SOMETHING

Retirement: When you stop living at work and start working at living.

IF SOMEONE VIEWS THEIR JOB or career as something they *do*, then it naturally follows that work is *done* upon retirement. But a better attitude is retiring TO something, rather than FROM something. Leaving a profession isn't just for the freedom to now do whatever you want. Without question, it's nice to spend time pursuing hobbies, traveling, and taking life at a slower pace. But leisure activities can't fill the remainder of your life.

Most theologians agree that the word "retirement" is not a biblical concept. At least not in the sense of quitting. When the Lord created Adam and Eve, what did God appoint for them to do? To work. And before the fall of man, work was considered good! It was an integral part of God's best plan for mankind.

Work keeps our minds sharp, our bodies moving and more importantly, lengthens our life. Extensive research shows that people who retire early tend to die sooner. One study from Oregon State University found that even people who considered themselves unhealthy lived longer if they kept working at a manageable pace. The study reported that healthy adults who worked one year past age 65 decreased their risk of death by eleven percent.

If work is good, then is retirement bad? Of course not. But look at the word itself–*Re*tirement. The prefix "RE" means to do something again, like repeat or reiterate. To retire comes from the root *'tirer,'* which means to draw upon. Retirement is a time when we once again appeal to or draw upon the Lord to obtain His *next* plan for our lives.

That plan may include travel. It will probably include some leisure. But it should never involve withdrawing from society into complete seclusion or retreat. God has a new plan, and it consists of using your experiences gained up to that moment. Now that your time is freed up from the constraints of a nine-to-five workday consider yourself blessed with opportunities to serve the Lord more fully.

Many retirees participate in mission trips or assist in ministry with their free time. Volunteerism by older adults is a tremendous benefit to many organizations. And it's a blessing for the volunteer, as well.

A study conducted by the Corporation for National and Community Service found that Americans over the age of 60 had fewer disabilities and higher levels of well-being when they volunteered of themselves to an outside organization. It gives you a sense of accomplishment and a reason to get up each day. It allows you to connect with other people. Donating your time and energy to a more significant cause will strengthen your health and bring new meaning to your life.

Some older adults focus on family in a more significant way, post-retirement. Becoming involved in the lives of your nieces, nephews, and grandchildren is a fantastic way to stay connected to the next generation.

Now I'm not suggesting that you become a built-in daycare. Babysitting your grandkids fulltime might *not* be an ideal plan. It is critical to have open, honest conversations with your adult children if that becomes an issue. I have known people who suffered in silence after feeling used when providing free childcare, following their retirement. Rather than building up resentment, the best solution is to determine a healthy balance for all parties concerned.

Conversely, quality time with grandchildren is absolutely critical, to share your influence and guidance. Personally, I love being with my "grands" mainly when we're laughing and sharing silly stories about their life and mine.

You may have heard of the little boy who sat on his grandfather's knee one day, as they read about Noah's ark.

The little boy asked, "Grandpa, were you in Noah's ark?"

"Goodness, no!" said the grandfather.

"Then how come you didn't drown when the flood came?" asked the boy.

No doubt, grandchildren will perceive us as old! But don't let that keep you from spending time with them.

It's important to pray for the children in your life, as well. I dedicate several hours a week to praying for my grandkids. You'll find that the more time you've spent hanging out with them in person, the more insight you've gained about their particular needs and how to direct your "behind-the-scenes" prayers for each of them.

Theologian John Wesley wrote, "God does nothing, except in answer to prayer." Never underestimate the value of your prayers for someone else. Carve out time in retirement to pray regularly for family, friends, and neighbors. That is a valuable role to play in blessing the lives of others.

There is a mistaken belief that we become less useful as we grow older. But life is a pilgrim's progression. Be it through prayer, volunteerism, ministry, or even childcare, trust that the Lord has new work for you. With each step, you are not moving away *from* a career or a previous place, but you are being led *to* a more incredible opportunity.

CHAPTER 16

NEVER STOP LEARNING

The excitement of learning separates youth from old age. As long as you're learning, you're not old. ROSALYN S. YALOW

I WAS A LITTLE SURPRISED at the most popular answer to a question on my survey that asked, *"Which statement best describes your outlook on life?"* As you see in Figure 1, "I will never stop learning" was chosen by 47% of the respondents, clueing into a significant factor about growing old: There is always knowledge to obtain.

While it may be hard to teach old dogs new tricks, medical science shows that people *can* and *should* continue to learn new things in their later years. The barrier is not the person's age when it comes to absorbing new ideas. It is mainly that people make a subconscious decision to stop learning somewhere along midlife.

By middle age, most people have studied long and hard to obtain the requirements necessary to advance in a career. Some have devoted many years in formal education, such as college or trade school, to complete the prerequisites for their profession. Others have attended the school of hard knocks to thoroughly learn an occupation that will support them. And after you gain a certain level of expertise in your job, formal learning then becomes optional (except perhaps the continuing education periodically required to maintain your license or credentials).

POSSIBLE ANSWERS	RESPONSES
I will never stop learning.	47%
Sixty is the new forty!	21%
My best days are out in front of me!	11%
I am the wisest I will ever be.	8%
I came, I saw, I conquered!	4%
I did it my way!	4%
I'm just a relic that needs to be put on a shelf.	4%
It's time for a new generation to rule the world.	2%
	100%

Figure 1: What Statement Best Describes Your Outlook on Life?

Did you know that nearly forty percent of all college graduates never read another book following school? Since books are so important to me and such a fun way to learn, that is almost beyond belief.

In today's fast paced world, if you're not learning, you're falling behind. You should never stop learning. I make an annual resolution to learn more about a hobby or pursue a new talent. It can be something small, like perfecting a bread recipe or growing tomatoes. At other times, it involves something bigger like mastering a computer program or moving to the next level in a piano series. But I always strive to learn.

Numerous studies provide valid reasons for learning a new skill or completing mental exercises, as you grow in age. Here are a few:

1. People who continuously learn are happier. When your focus is centered on absorbing something new, it keeps you energized. Have you ever lost track of time, while learning a new hobby or reading an interesting book, because you were thoroughly enjoying it? Engagement in mental activity brings the benefit of happiness.

2. Your capacity for knowledge is tremendous. Your brain can hold the equivalent of three million hours of TV shows. It would take over 300 years with the TV continually running to use up all that storage. Scientists estimate that our brain could also retain the information printed in over 4 million books. People use much less of their brain's total capacity than is possible.

3. Knowledge isn't fixed or constant. The volume of information available within this world increases every second. To live your life without ongoing study causes you to become static and stuck in the past. If you want to carry on relevant conversations with young people, become familiar with the latest technology or current pop culture. In Isaiah 43:19, the prophet expresses that God is doing "new things," and we need to perceive them.

4. Your brain needs to be fed and exercised. Expanding your knowledge is necessary to maintain critical thinking. A ten-year study found that people who continue to learn can significantly reduce their risk of dementia. Cognitive exercise

also helps a person sustain their brain's processing speed and their ability to manage complex information.
5. Although the brain is an organ, it works like a muscle with the "use it or lose it" principle. Regular stimulation from art, music, reading, and socializing helps to preserve your mental health.

Knowledge is obtained through a mixture of three distinct learning styles of learning:

VISUAL learners retain information best when they read or see it through printed words, graphs, and charts.

AUDITORY learners respond to information that is reinforced with sound. They gather information by listening to lectures, seminars, music, and books on tape.

KINESTHETIC learners remember information through a hands-on approach. Lab experiments and other tactile work helps them retain knowledge.

As a simple illustration, consider what you do when trying out a new recipe, which involves both visual and kinesthetic learning. You read the printed recipe (visual learning) and use your hands to prepare it (kinesthetic learning). The combination of both learning styles aids in retaining the knowledge of how to make that exact dish the next time around!

Young adults typically respond more favorably to a particular learning style. However, as we age, our preferred method of learning may change. As a young student sitting in a classroom, you may have assimilated information primarily by hearing it. Yet later in life, you now prefer to read printed information about a specific subject.

Older age can bring physical limitations, as well. Decreased hearing, diminished eyesight, or loss of mobility compounds your ability to learn in the same way as you did in the past. For mature adults, learning through a combination of two or more methods is most effective.

Let's say you have difficulty tracking a conversation because of hearing loss. It would be difficult to completely absorb information that was *only* presented in lecture form. However, you could read a printed script from the presentation, and combine that with a hands-on activity that supports what is being taught, to fully comprehend a new concept.

I read about a lady that most people have never known, but who is an inspiration for us all. Up until 2019, Nola Ochs was in the Guinness Book of World Records as the oldest person to graduate with a master's degree. She studied at Fort Hays State University and earned this title in 2010 at the ripe old age of 98 years! Nola was honored on the Jay Leno show as the oldest college graduate ever and given a nine-day cruise to take along with her granddaughter who graduated at the same time.

Nola started college back in 1930 but had to stop short of her bachelor's degree to raise her children and work on the family farm. In 2007, she picked up where she had left off and completed both her bachelor's and master's degrees within just a few years. As of her 100th birthday, she was working as a Graduate Teaching Assistant. And Nola continued to work until her death in 2016.

We are blessed to live in a nation where we are free to learn at any age. And we have many options available to acquire knowledge. For one, you may choose distance-learning to keep your mind sharp. Numerous sites online offer courses, classes, and even degrees for older adults.

Learning via the internet provides the flexibility to study at your own pace and the ability to replay lessons if something was missed during the first pass. Copies of lecture notes are typically posted for students, as well.

Online learning is generally more affordable, particularly for people on fixed incomes, e.g., retirees.

The main point is this: Growing old is never a reason to stop acquiring knowledge. The Bible says in Psalm 92:14, "They shall still bear fruit in old age; they shall be fresh and flourishing." One of the best ways to stay relevant in an ever-changing world is through continued learning. Though our bodies may decline, education brings many positive benefits that allow our minds to thrive.

CHAPTER 17

WHAT TO DO WHEN YOU'RE FEELING OLD

You can't help growing older, but you don't have to be old. GEORGE BURNS

A PRIMARY GOAL of this book is to encourage mature adults to believe they are relevant to this world. Even after leaving accomplished careers and achieving great success, God still has a purpose that only you can fill. If you're still breathing, God has designs for you. The Bible says in Ephesians 1:11 that He is working out His purpose in everything and in everyone. Everyone includes you—at age 12 or at age 92.

Yet there are days when you just feel old and irrelevant. Being "old" is a state of mind associated with the negative results of aging. Arthritic joints, sickness, and the frailty of the human body can reinforce false notions that we are less significant, as we age. The world places such value on youth and energy that we mistakenly view gray hair and wrinkles as characteristics to fix, rather than embrace.

Granted, I'm making myself a little vulnerable here, but I've often been caught up in the flaws of my age, and it's not fun, nor productive. It is easy to get side-tracked from your abilities and purpose when you focus on the downsides of aging.

A few years back, I realized a somewhat destructive pattern in my daily routine when waking up each morning and viewing myself in the mirror. Let me elaborate.

I started with a "wrinkle-check" on my face. *Hum? Was that line there last week? Wow, there's another one. My goodness! Hey, wait. Is that spot new? Wonder if there's a product to minimize those droopy bags under my eyes. And speaking of eyes, it may be time to have that cataract examined. There were a few floaters last night when driving home.*

Then I moved to the hair. *I'd better schedule a color appointment soon; there are too many gray hairs popping out. I look like a skunk with that new growth showing. Maybe I'll try a different style. This long hair might be pulling down the overall appearance of my face.*

And finally, on to the teeth. *Are these things shifting? It's messing up my smile. Who would believe I wore braces all those years? Oh, maybe today I'll call that lady who mentioned there's a new miracle tooth whitener on the market. It might be worth a shot.*

This very unproductive process consumed the first few minutes of the morning, as I pondered my reflection. Every. Single. Day.

All of us want to be the best we can be. And while coloring your hair or using a wrinkle cream won't throw the world off its axis, a person cannot become consumed in their later years with remedies to turn back the clock. We all know people who will use any physical means necessary to reverse aging through the latest technologies, treatments, and surgeries. But to my knowledge, no one has ever discovered the Fountain of Youth.

And then some totally ignore the physical signs of aging, with the hope that no one will notice. It's sad to admit that I've concealed a smile now and then when feeling self-conscious about my shifting teeth.

One of the things I was most interested to learn from the survey was what other people do when they are feeling the sting of age. Perhaps there were more productive ideas available than a critical daily review of myself in the mirror!

"When I'm feeling old or outdated, I typically..." was presented as a multiple-choice question, listing some presumed answers. But respondents were also given the option to provide an alternative suggestion. And not surprisingly, many people offered creative thoughts about what *they* do when feeling old or insignificant.

The most popular answers are displayed in Figure 1 and provide ideas you might try if you come into a place of discouragement regarding your physical age.

POSSIBLE ANSWERS	RESPONSES
Turn to prayer, reflection, contemplation	38%
Retreat in silence	16%
Change something about my appearance	12%
Take up a new sport or hobby	8%
Other	7%
I don't ever feel old	6%
Buy something "young"	6%
Learn something new	5%
Exercise	3%
	100%

Figure 1: Survey Responses to the Question "When I'm feeling old or outdated, I typically:"

Some respondents shared that when they feel outdated, they "push through" or simply "deal with it." *(*There's that *"pedal on through the curves"* theory being reinforced once again!*)* A few people stated that a glass of wine each evening helps settle concerns about wrinkles and achy joints. Long naps, time with grandchildren and good books do the trick, as well as playing on Facebook and watching TV. But there may be more to it, than that.

Feeling old or outdated may be a symptom of spiritual distress. Your old soul may have a tired spirit. A broken dream or unfulfilled expectation, festering deep in your soul, may need God's healing touch. For several months after leaving my fulltime career, I experienced periods of loneliness and low self-esteem. A dark shadow of gloom followed me like a cloud. My goals and ambitions had been interrupted, and I was lost as to where to head next.

After visiting with a Christian counselor, he recommended some excellent advice to heed when feeling unimportant. To summarize his words, I've lightheartedly sorted his recommendations into three simple concepts: play, pray and stay (the course).

PLAY.

My Uncle Don is an active 90-year-old man. Being tall in stature, basketball has always been his favorite recreational activity. For over 70 years, Uncle Don has regularly played and/or coached basketball, at least twice a week.

Growing up, our families lived in the same town and visited regularly. His energy and enthusiasm were always impressive. But after moving to different states, we lost touch except through social media. It was sad to read his most recent Facebook post where Uncle Don announced he was leaving his senior basketball team after twenty-two years of participation.

The team had traveled from coast to coast, competing in state and national tournaments over the last two decades. His team had also made it twice to the Senior Olympics, winning the gold medal one year and silver in yet another.

But in recent years, due to illness, injury, and death, his team had dwindled down to only five players. My uncle shared that it had become increasingly challenging to stay competitive and maintain the schedule, with such few players. And now his own health was declining, and so he was "retiring" from basketball, at 90 years old!

Uncle Don's life is an excellent example of what to do when you're feeling old. When asked what he would tell someone younger, my uncle offered his best advice, "Stay active."

The word "play" is from the Old English *pleg* "to exercise," and is also related to the word "dance" or "leap for joy." The emphasis here is on leaping and moving forward through exercise, or by working out. Any activity, be it physical or mental, that keeps you utilizing your body, is play. Whether you exercise your mind through reading and playing board games or your body through mountain climbing and skydiving, it is crucial to regularly participate in something that moves you onward and brings joy to your soul.

Play also provides rest. A playful activity should be geared for recreation and restoration. Why do you often see retirees on the golf course, on tennis courts, or in a comfortable library chair? Because these interests bring enjoyment and help you relax.

Let's not overlook people who live with limitations. You may not have the physical agility for *any* sport, let alone to play basketball well into your later years. Disability and disease often restrict a person's ability to keep their bodies moving physically. Consider singing, playing guitar, sewing, or fishing, which all bring joy without the need for vigorous intensity.

In recent years many traditionally rigorous sports like volleyball, cycling, and basketball have been modified to accommodate people with physical disabilities. These adaptive activities give people with limited mobility the opportunity to maintain their coordination and body strength.

You may have heard the term "child's play," which refers to a task that is easy to do or perhaps even petty. Sadly, as we age, it can become increasingly difficult to include even trivial forms of play into our schedule.

But it's no small matter for seniors to find outlets to keep moving forward in joy. Playing aids your health, and it's a blessing for your soul. Most importantly, it keeps you from being old. PLAY!

PRAY.

A while back, someone told me, "Anytime I feel outdated, I do something to rectify the situation." That got me thinking, how *do* we rectify old age?

To rectify means to set or make something right by making some adjustments. The word originates from the Latin root *rectus* or "straight." And prayer is our straight, direct line of access to God.

It is a time when you close out the noise of the world and make things right with Him. Through prayer, give the unfulfilled dreams, bad choices, and poor decisions of the past to God. I John 1:9 says that "If we confess our sins, He is faithful and just to forgive them."

Prayer and reflection are critical to obtaining peace of mind when combating discouragement about your life and purpose. Rather than concentrating on yourself, as I admitted to doing every day in the mirror, prayer adjusts your focus outward toward God. It keeps you humble before Him and reminds you that you're not in control, but He is. I didn't create myself, and I only exist because God wills that I exist. Through prayer, our heavenly Father reveals to us the reason for being and the objectives of our current purpose.

Prayer equates to someone stopping and asking for directions. If you don't know where the road of life is taking you next, ask the Lord to guide you with each step. Don't drive around mindlessly throughout your remaining days.

It's not spiritually healthy to start each day by looking into the mirror with worry about your wrinkles and flaws. Greet the Lord your maker each morning with excitement, embracing His perfect plan for where the road will take you on that particular day.

Allow me to share my *new* routine when looking at my image in the mirror. It's more of a prayer than an assessment of my flaws.

Dear Lord, I'm so thankful that I have eyes to see my reflection here today. And I have spiritual vision to see beyond these wrinkles and lines. They are small indicators of the beautiful journey that you've brought me on so far. And I'm excited about the trip that is mine for this day. Thank you that my lungs are taking in breath and my heart is beating, and I'm alive because of you. With long life, You will satisfy me on this earth.

Thank you that I have a divine assignment this day, and You will give me everything I need to accomplish it. I give you my mind and ask You to keep it free from the anxieties and cares of life, so that I may think like You. Because through your Holy Spirit, I have the mind of Christ.

As David wrote in the Psalms, You have taught me from my youth and You will not forsake me as I age. And for that, I bless Your name. Amen.

Every. Single. Day. PRAY!

STAY (the course).
Even as we grow in years, we should be furthering the kingdom of God. It is not someone else's job or responsibility to accomplish this. He has entrusted each of us with individual gifts that assist the body of Christ. Some teach. Some give. Some offer counsel. That's why it is called a "community" of faith. Because each of us has a divine impartation on our life that is to be shared with others.

Every so often, I come across someone winding down their life and find that they have relaxed in exercising their spiritual gifts, as well. This is true, particularly when it comes to your church home. When you were young, were you a giver? Then why stop being a giver now that you're older? If you were a gifted teacher or administrator, don't cease sharing those blessings with your congregation.

Last year, I had the privilege of working with a delightful "young" lady named Pat. I joke when referring to her as young because in actuality she had just celebrated her 80th birthday when we met. All kidding aside, Pat is the perfect example of what I hope my life looks like when I am her age.

While working on a church remodel project together, she and I had to meet regularly to discuss the execution of our plans. You need to know that Pat's days are tirelessly filled with classes, lectures, trips, and Bible studies. So, when we would compare our calendars to schedule those on-going meetings, it was always more difficult for *her* to find a blank spot, then it was for me. She's the most involved 80-year old I've ever met!

Pat has taught me to "keep on, keeping on" when it comes to exercising your spiritual gifts. If you have been blessed with the gift of organization, then use that talent today to reduce the clutter in a Sunday school classroom or on a friend's closet. If you were formerly a handyman, continue repairing and restoring items that require attention. The church needs *all* people to work collectively, using the abilities given to them, to further the kingdom of God.

As a former college professor of Nursing, Pat understands the importance of keeping her mind sharp and of continuing to learn. She has used her gifts to host wellness conferences and various other continuing education activities at her church. She doesn't think, "Let someone else do it now. I've done it for years, and I'm tired." Pat allows the Lord to use the gifts and experiences of her past, right here in the present, to impact the future of many others.

A local paper recently featured an article about a 90-year old woman who is a talented artist. Over the years, she has painted numerous portraits of well-known people in her community and state, even working at one point as a sketch artist for local police. She has the gift of capturing the actual likeness and unique expressions of a person on canvas. Her reputation has spread internationally throughout her career, and a few years ago she was commissioned to complete a painting of an Italian priest, to be given as a birthday present to Pope John Paul II.

After losing her husband twenty years ago, friends and relatives expected this amazing lady to retire from her art. But she told them, "I will never quit. You never stop using the gifts that God gave you." Like my friend Pat, this artist models the behavior of one who has continued to operate in their God-given abilities and to remain worthwhile to the world. STAY (the course)!

* * *

We can't stop the hands of time as life marches on. The years take their toll on our bodies, reducing our strength, coordination, fine motor skills—even our reaction time. These are external forces to be dealt with.

But at any age, we must refuse to be "old" in the sense that we cease being who God created us to be. When you're feeling your age: Play, pray, and stay the course!

PART FIVE

LIVING LIFE OUTSIDE OF A BOX

CHAPTER 18

MENTORING THEM FOR SUCCESS

Even when I am old and gray, do not forsake me, my God, until I declare your power to the next generation, your mighty acts to all who are to come. PSALM 71:18

THE EXPERIENCE, knowledge, or wisdom gained over a person's lifetime, isn't for them alone. It is to be shared. In Chapter 2 of Titus, the Bible instructs that one of the duties of older women is to encourage young women. Older men are implored to teach all, as is his responsibility. Both the young and the old, men and women, preachers and servants are all to conduct themselves accordingly and to fulfill their *duties*.

What are the duties of older persons, as used in this context? One such role is that of mentoring. Younger people need encouragement, training, and support. The word of God is timeless and universal; it pertains to everyone. But in today's world, people of younger generations don't always know God's word or how to apply it to their life. The noise of worldly philosophies can easily drown out the solid Christian principles that we were created to live by.

The word "mentor" correlates to a wise and trusted counselor in Scripture. This is where older people become invaluable. A person in their later years has been prepared to inspire others who are not yet at that same place in life. God desires that each generation pass on knowledge and guidance to the next.

Judges 2:10 reads, "After that whole generation had been gathered to their fathers, another generation grew up, who knew neither the Lord, not what He had done for Israel." How sad to know that an entire generation did not know the Lord or what He had done for the nation of Israel. This likely happened because the first generation never passed on their experience or wisdom to the next. They simply lived their own lives and kept the knowledge of God to themselves.

Or, possibly the younger Israelites didn't want to hear the instruction of their predecessors. It is imperative that the one being mentored be receptive. A closed mind and heart can cut off the blessings to be gained from wisdom. You cannot lead someone who doesn't want to follow. But when someone is hungry, they need to be fed. Always pray that God will open doors of opportunities for you to share with others.

Don't be intimidated about encouraging others in the Lord. Anyone who teaches another learns as well. Growing in years brings the patience, confidence, and faith needed to withstand the trials of life. Why would you be hesitant to share this with someone younger who could benefit from your clearer understanding?

As you grow in years, consider that there will always be someone younger than you who needs your support. Not through money and time necessarily, but through a word of encouragement or as a cheerleader in their time of trial. You cannot walk someone else's journey. But you can reinforce the understanding that they will make it through *their* tests, with *your* life as a testimony.

How did Jesus mentor his disciples? He did so by telling them to "follow me." That is the real objective of mentoring, following the example of another. If you have seen proven success in any area of your life, allow someone to mirror your footsteps. Train them to model their behaviors and strategies after you, to move toward the same outcome.

The apostle, Paul, was an excellent example of godly mentorship. Except for Jesus, there was no other person in the Bible who possessed such a forward-thinking vision for ministry. Paul served as a mentor to Timothy and described himself and this young man as "like-minded," even comparing their relationship to that of a father and son. Years before, when Paul was a new Christian, he, too, had benefited from the leadership and example of his mentor, Barnabas.

In his letter to the church at Philippi, he wrote, "Brothers and sisters together, follow my example and copy those who live the way we modeled it for you." (Phil. 3:17, EXB). But Paul knew that the achievements attained in his ministry depended on the hand of God to lead and guide. He humbly implored the Corinthian church to "Follow my example, as I follow the example of Christ." (1 Cor. 11:1 NKJ) Like Paul, we must always be ready to ask someone to follow us, *as we follow Christ*.

Accountability is required for mentoring. We must be the best example and role model when we help direct someone else's journey. Even when our outer man is decaying, our inner man should be continually renewed in hope, in love and in faith in Christ. One role we have as Christian believers is to share what the Lord has done for us with future generations.

Mentoring brings joy to a person in their later years. It comes from knowing that you have played a part in boosting the life of someone who has fallen. Mentoring produces satisfaction in recognizing that your life experiences were lived so that you might help others. As you mature in your faith, others grow with you and because of you.

All generations have different lessons to pass on. There is much to be gained from those who have walked before us. The Lord places people in your path—church members, neighbors, relatives—who can provide a higher perspective to your life, by sharing examples from theirs.

You may not realize that some of the most successful people in the last century have sought the assistance of a mentor. Bill Gates, a Microsoft co-founder, often refers to Warren Buffett, businessman, and investor, as his mentor. Steve Jobs, founder of Apple, Inc. mentored Mark Zuckerberg, co-founder of Facebook, for many years.

Sally Ride, first American woman to travel into space, had worked for years prior under her mentor Dr. Arthur Walker. She credits her historical achievements to having a person like Dr. Walker believe in her. Sir Richard Branson, the founder of the Virgin Group, said, "If you ask any successful businessperson, they will always say that they have had a great mentor at some point along the road." Has God placed someone on the same road as you, for this purpose?

Living your life as a model for others is a principle that impacts generations. It has a profound influence on both the present and the future. Pray that the Holy Spirit will open doors for you to make yourself available to a person who will benefit from your spiritual journey. Determine to become invested in their personal and spiritual growth so that they may reach their full potential.

CHAPTER 19

PREPARE TO LEAVE A LEGACY

Our fingerprints don't fade from the lives we touch. JUDY BLUME

DYING REMOVES YOUR PHYSICAL PRESENCE from the earth. But your beliefs, principles, and achievements should live on in the hearts of the people you have touched. It is the responsibility of every person to create and leave a legacy for the next generation.

You don't have to be a millionaire or a land baron to accomplish this, because a legacy involves more than an inheritance of wealth and personal property. It is the passing on of principles, experiences, and meaningful knowledge that will aid future generations in becoming better people.

For example, if you are a grandparent, you have the blessed opportunity to model the heritage of living for Jesus Christ to your grandchildren. Proverbs 13:22 says that "a good man leaves an inheritance to his children's children." A spiritual legacy is one that far outlasts money or possessions.

I cannot stress enough that there is a special bond between a grandparent and a grandchild. And you have influence over who they will become. Rather than bearing the responsibility of training and disciplining your grandchildren, you can hug them, accept them, and instill value in them. Grandparents always know the right things to say at just the right time. There may be children in your proximity who don't have a blood relative living anywhere near them and need your advice as a surrogate grandparent.

Teach your grandkids about Jesus and to value God's word. Share your legacy of faith with them. Pray that they will come to know God at a young age and serve Him all the days of their life. The blessings in your life today are likely the result of a grandparent who prayed for *you* when you were young!

Over the years, I have visited with many who are literally at death's door and who want the assurance they are leaving something behind that will outlive their existence. Some people point to the children they have influenced over the years. Some ponder their years of service to a church or local charity. Others reflect on the examples they set in their workplace. We all hope to have contributed something significant to the world we shared.

For nearly fifteen years, I worked in the funeral home industry. Do you know one of the toughest tasks involved in arranging the funeral of a loved one? It is writing a person's obituary. Yes, newspapers have boilerplate forms where you can easily plug in facts to create a suitable bio; but this can be impersonal.

Instead, people are opting to write creative and touching tributes that capture the unique character of their friend or relative. They choose not to draft a few short paragraphs, summarizing one's *entire* life. What you'll find attached to an obituary nowadays is a message of purpose, i.e., what their loved one has left behind for others to carry forward.

Have you considered what you want to be expressed in the final words concerning your life? Would you encourage people not to sweat the small stuff? Would you remind them to spend more time with their family? Would you advise them to eat better or exercise more?

When you are young, you don't think about this kind of advice because leaving a legacy seems so far away. But here's the thing: Even though your life's message is ultimately preserved through the words of an obituary or epitaph, your legacy *commenced* years before. Your legacy originated the moment you entered into adulthood.

In *7 Habits of Highly Effective People*, author Stephen Covey proposed that if you want to develop a vision on how to live your life, you should visualize attending your *own* funeral. This concept may make you a little uncomfortable, but it helps you discover the importance of living with the intent to leave a legacy.

Covey says to picture the day when family and friends will gather to commemorate your life. They will share memories, tell stories, and reminisce about you. What do you want them to say? What characteristics do you hope they will have observed in you? What will they have learned from watching you walk through the trials and circumstances of life?

This mental exercise aids in building a vision for your life's potential. Once you determine that vision, you'll map your life accordingly. Years from now, if you want to be remembered for your kindness, you will seek to be kind today. If you hope to be remembered as wise, you will live wisely in the present. And, so on and so on!

Your heritage begins with a clear and distinct purpose and develops over the years. With the Lord's help, you determine what is most important and then start moving toward that. And you press on toward the mark.

A legacy isn't only about being remembered during a memorial service. It begins as a decision to model a particular behavior or to live by a guiding belief, which in turn is *passed on* to others and then endures through generations. Think of this as your gift to the people who love you; something for them to remember you by.

It's not a strategic plan or a set of goals that we hope to meet. As American businessman Max Depree wrote in *Leading Without Power: Finding Hope in Serving Community*, a legacy is "the cumulative informal record of how close we came, to the person we intended to be." It isn't what you *planned* to accomplish over your life. It is the behavior and principles you actually demonstrated over time and then handed on.

As I mentioned before, my father was a minister. He dedicated his life to leading people into the Christian faith. He was a confident man who witnessed to store clerks, bank tellers, and anyone else who would listen. Often, I would be embarrassed by his bold approach, but God had dramatically changed my father's life for the better when he was a young man, and Dad was very serious about his faith.

One winter evening, when I was a teenager, my family sat at a local restaurant, laughing and sharing together. During our conversation, my dad, who was 38 at the time, mentioned that he felt his life wouldn't last much longer. It was a shocking comment; he didn't have a terminal illness or any reason to make such a statement. But he was sincere about his feelings. Naturally, this unnerved my mom, and she asked him to stop being morbid.

I clearly remember my father saying, "Oh, I'm not afraid to die. And I'm going to make the most of my life while I'm here. But I just have a feeling I won't live a long life."

On the very next day, Dad's life was cut short by a drunk driver who had been excessively celebrating New Year's Eve. Our family never expected, that on a fateful Sunday afternoon while taking a leisurely ride to visit grandparents, someone would veer into our lane and end my father's life and ministry in a matter of seconds. My eight-year-old brother died that day, as well. Neither of them had the opportunity to become all that God had ordained for their lives on earth.

There have been times when I longed for just 24 more hours with my father. Over the years, I have wanted to hear his uproarious laugh once again or listen to him share stories about his childhood. He would have loved knowing my husband and spoiling his grandchildren.

While our days together were short, I am so thankful that my father understood the role of leaving an inheritance and that he left our family the legacy of serving Jesus Christ. I possess his passion for people, his organizational skills, and his use of humor to encourage others. His death brought the realization that life is precious and is a gift from God. And for that, I am grateful.

As humans, we are mortal. Our days will one day come to an end. There are no guarantees for a lengthy lifespan.

Do not wait until your dying moment to consider the meaning of life. Don't allow your time to draw to a close before understanding that the way you live today impacts those around you and their future. An essential task for you today is to consider what behaviors and principles will live on through you. If you've been blessed by a guiding truth, then share those blessings with others. Begin each day with the end in mind!

CHAPTER 20

MAPPING OUT THE NEXT TEN YEARS

The best time to plant a tree was twenty years ago. The second-best time is now.
CHINESE PROVERB

AS WE'VE LEARNED, the life you create after retirement will be your "Third Chapter" or the next act in life's performance. And understand this: You have a clean slate to write the script for this next act, including the direction you will take, the activities you'll participate in and the disciplines you will observe to maintain your health, wealth, and self.

But if you fail to prepare *in advance* for this third chapter, you may find yourself lost and living without purpose when the time comes. In interviewing new retirees, I've heard over and over that those first few weeks after leaving work become a time to decompress and find your sea legs. And that is critical to a successful transition. After all, for over half of your life, you've traded your time for the benefits of a job.

After interviewing some *newly retired* people, I found that some became dizzy and disoriented after leaving fulltime work. Their new days flew by quickly, and they came to realize they had nothing to show for it because they had failed to create a vision of what retirement would look like for them. Being retired doesn't mean you no longer follow a plan, set a goal, or make a list. Managing your time in this stage is as essential as it was during the days of working nine-to-five.

You've heard it said, "If you aim for nothing, you'll probably reach it." Aiming for something is a critical step, even on your toughest days, because it keeps you moving. You need to map out the road to your next performance before the time comes!

Failing to create a dream for your early retirement years could also cause you to become like a broken record, stuck in repetitive behavior or habits. For instance, if you have workaholic tendencies now, you might be prone to overschedule when entering this new stage. When I left the corporate world, I was so accustomed to a jam-packed daily agenda, it was a challenge to not fill up my *new* schedule with work-like activities. The drawers can only be so organized, and the pantry rearranged only to a reasonable extent! Work won't ever stop if you don't.

Some survey respondents, who were already living in retirement, provided insight for those of us still living in the second-to-the-last box. Repeatedly they shared a recommendation to create a plan during midlife, to ensure that the undertakings within your next act will be fulfilling and gratifying.

Life Coaches often advise people to create a ten-year master plan once you reach your fifties. Now that doesn't mean your life will come to an end after that, or once you retire! It's merely a manageable length of time for someone to attain reasonable goals.

Will you be starting a new business? Or learning a new talent? Will you be exploring uncharted territory or checking items off your bucket list?

Think about where you are now, and where you'd like to go from here as you approach your senior years. Create a primary objective for each of the categories listed next. Determine each of the steps necessary to achieve each goal.

- Financial
- Personal Health
- Personal Well-Being
- Family
- Spiritual
- Home
- Travel

For example, if you want to update your home over the next ten years, set that as your chief ambition for the "Home" category. Then construct a timeline to repaint, repair, and/or replace what is needed. List out each significant task or expenditure necessary to complete your home remodel plan.

You might discover the need to adjust your strategy for completing one objective if it conflicts with your ability to complete another. Work through the plan until the proportions feel right. Adjust along the way, as needed. You'll find in your later years that flexibility is vital, so go with the flow.

Along those same lines, when forming a financial plan for this next act make a list of the critical items you *must* do and a list of the non-essential things you'd *like* to do.

Separate the needs from the wants. Decide which items will genuinely add value to your life and then determine what you really want.

Experts suggest that everyone has a list of approximately 10-15 regular everyday needs required to sustain them (e.g., a dependable car, a television, or a washer and dryer). But very few people have the time *and* the money to check off every need and every want on their list. It's necessary to find the right balance.

There is nothing wrong with focusing on your wants from time-to-time. They are an essential part of life and can be a great reward to motivate you. But don't allow those extras to steer you off course or drain your budget. Many people treat themselves to luxury items during midlife because of their increased income. Just remember to stay informed and make quality investments while in this stage of higher earnings.

Here are some additional things to consider when plotting out a course for the upcoming stage of life:

- Be realistic. If you've let some to-do's pile up over the years by putting them off until you have more time, don't expect to tackle them all at once following your retirement. The truth is, it'll all get done in the end. (*And if it doesn't, it probably wasn't as necessary as you thought!*)
- Create the right mix of structure and leisure. Maintain the proper equilibrium for your own well-being. Incorporate learning, recreation, volunteerism, hobbies, travel, and time with family and friends into the equation.
- Take a few risks! If you've always wanted to visit Australia, but the long flights have deterred you, plan to go for it. Take the risk or lose the opportunity.

- Once retired, find your new rhythm. Without the need to "clock in" every morning, you will own the schedule. If you tend to be more productive in the evening, then build your day accordingly. You'll no longer be constrained to a forty-hour workweek. If you want to attend a movie during the day and tackle housework at night, so be it. Seek to create a cadence that allows you to rest, but also to remain productive.

Most importantly, trust God to guide your plans. The Bible says, "Commit your plans to the Lord, and He will make [cause] them to succeed." (Prov. 16:3) God will work behind the scenes to align favor and good breaks to come your way when you release your faith to Him.

The word "commit" means to completely give over. And the Hebrew word "make" in this passage means to establish. That is, God will bring your plans about, in His perfect way and in His perfect time, when you give them entirely to Him.

Years ago, we knew a man named Dan, who was in his early sixties. He had worked at an oil company for many years and was considered an expert in his field. He loved his job, although it required extensive travel during the week.

Although Dan had worked ever since leaving college, he had experienced some unfortunate circumstances over the years, which left him living paycheck to paycheck and trapped in a mountain of debt, with no end in sight. He felt that retirement just "wasn't in the cards" for him. He had no vision for his future and couldn't picture a world that included anything other than work to provide a living.

Dan's wife fell into poor health and was diagnosed with a terminal illness. He needed to reduce his long work hours to be with her, but he didn't have a solution. He shared how one day when he had lost all hope, he gave the entire situation to God. He asked the Lord for the *time* and the *means* to be with his wife in her final years. Although Dan didn't see an answer, God did.

Unbeknownst to Dan, his company was being acquired through a merger. And just a few weeks after crying out to the Lord for help, Dan was offered a generous severance package making it possible for him to retire, debt-free. God made a way where there was no way. And our friend was able to spend the next few years caring fulltime for his wife. Following her death, Dan went on to discover new ways to find fulfillment and joy outside of work.

The word "plan" comes from the Latin, *planus*, which means to level. God doesn't want your life to be a constant uphill battle. Proverbs 3:6 says, "In all your ways acknowledge Him, and He will make your paths straight." To rephrase this, God will level the ground for your journey as you commit your plans to Him. He promises to give you what is needed to navigate through the road ahead.

Life is *absolutely* a journey, not a destination. If you are in the middle of your journey, believe that there are still many exciting adventures to be experienced on the path before you.

And be mindful of this: If you were taking a cross-country expedition, you would pack and prepare in advance. You would make time to research what is needed and to map out exactly where you were headed. You'd ensure that you had everything required to safely arrive at your destination and to guarantee the success of your trip.

Why make a trek into your senior years without doing the same? Ask God to direct your steps in preparing for the next chapter of your life. Rely on His Holy Spirit to give you realistic ideas and level ground to walk on, as you make future plans. Then trust Him to bless the next ten years with opportunities to fulfill these dreams through His unmerited favor.

CHAPTER 21

DOING THE OLD THINGS IN A NEW WAY

When God begins to do a new thing in a new way, the greatest opposition comes from the old thing with its old ways.
LISA BEVERE

AS YOU GROW OLDER, it becomes harder to embrace anything new. You become more comfortable with the old way, whether it refers to your looks, your habits, or your view of the world. At the very beginning of this book, I mentioned how my grandfather would say "Back in my day" when he commented about anything new. Human nature tricks us into believing that the old approach is always better.

For instance, I recently purchased a new phone. My *old* phone was working fine, but my grandchildren told me it was an outdated model. The salesman confirmed this by explaining that my phone, which was six years old, was four versions behind in technology and their company no longer supported it. So, after much deliberation, I walked out of the store with the latest, greatest phone available on the market. *After all, it would probably be another six years before purchasing my next one!*

But here's the point: I was very comfortable with the old phone. It made calls and received texts and stored pictures. What else is a phone supposed to do? It wasn't as if the new one was going to wash the dishes for me! I was just tired of hearing my family complain about my antiquated phone.

When I pull out the new phone, people say, "Oh, you've got the such-and-such model. Wow! That's really nice." Which is surprising to me, because the old one never garnered those type of comments. And I've watched videos and googled instructions, and now several days later, I'm still trying to figure out how to use this silly thing. Yesterday, I had a fleeting thought: *Should I just pull that old phone out of the toy box and charge it back up? It was so easy to use and a lot less stressful!*

Coincidentally, today I'm penning the information for *this* chapter, which as you can see is a teaching on doing old things in a new way. Life has its ironies, doesn't it? I'm reminded of a story in the second chapter of Mark about old and new things.

To provide some background, in Jesus' day, several religious traditions had long been observed within the Jewish faith. For example, fasting was a firmly established ritual, practiced for generations by a sect of Jews known as the Pharisees. This group was meticulous about observing laws and traditions, especially when it came to eating, tithing, and purity.

In this passage in Mark, we read about an occasion when Jesus (*the Messiah that the Jews were waiting for*) had been teaching and sharing a meal with certain people that the Pharisees would never have been around—sinners and tax collectors. And Jesus was doing this while the Pharisees were observing a fast. So, they were very disturbed, first because Jesus and his disciples were *eating* and also because they were eating with *sinners*. The Pharisees piously asked the disciples, "Why are we fasting, but you aren't?"

It's ironic that the Pharisees never thought, "Hey, this guy might be the one we're waiting for." On more than one occasion, they had observed throngs of people who hung on every word that Jesus taught. But the Pharisees were so religious and stuck in their ways that they wouldn't allow Jesus to be part of their culture or even entertain the thought that He might be the Messiah. They were entrenched in fasting and religious orders and couldn't embrace Jesus and his contemporary ideas. They preferred the old because they didn't get the new.

Jesus gave an answer to their question in the form of a parable; one that sheds light on the challenge of welcoming anything new. In Mark 2:22, Jesus said, "No one puts new wine into old wineskins. If he does, the wine will burst the skins and the wine will be destroyed, along with the skins. But new wine is for fresh wineskins."

In those days, water was often too contaminated to drink, and so wine was the primary beverage. The wine was stored in a vessel fashioned from the skin of a goat which had been sewn in such a way as to make it totally watertight. As the grape juice fermented within those containers, the goatskin would dry out and harden. Once the wine was removed from that old wineskin, you couldn't add more juice back into it because it would burst, i.e., a previously used wine vessel couldn't be reused once it had dried out.

Jesus was essentially saying, "Don't try to put your old beliefs in the new system. I'm the sacrifice going forward, as the lamb of God. Your religious ways won't work anymore. They are dried out. You don't have to go to a priest to be one with God now. I came to give you a new belief system and a new perspective. I'm replacing the old wineskin."

As we grow older, it becomes harder and harder to change. New things bring fear and anxiety to older folks. Even if the new is better, the old makes us feel secure. You may have heard the phrase, "The devil we know is better than the devil we don't."

Most of us don't like it when a new way doesn't work like the old. We avoid change because we are hesitant to let go. Personally, I had come to a point where I would have preferred to go back several iterations in phone technology than learn the advantages of my new model. I couldn't let go of what I had known.

Like I mentioned previously, moving around a lot as a pastor's daughter was difficult because I didn't like change. But a truth I learned as a young believer, is recorded in the book of Isaiah, chapter 43, and has always brought me peace. In verses 18 and 19, we read, "Don't consider the things of old. I am doing a new thing. Do you not perceive it?"

God is saying here, "I'm doing something totally new and completely different. Be aware of it." He doesn't say, "I'm going to *improve* your life and *update* the old." He says that He's doing something entirely new, not even resembling what it was before.

2 Corinthians 5:17 says, "If anyone is in Christ, He [or she] is a new creation. The old has gone, the new is here!" Notice it doesn't say, he or she is an "improved" creation or a better version of what they were. It means an entirely new creation.

Think about this: What new thing does God want to do in your life? Try not to name something that you want to improve or readjust. What brand new concept or idea do you want to start perceiving? You've got to let go of the old wine and the old container for God to fill you with something new.

A couple of years ago, country singer Toby Keith was playing golf with actor Clint Eastwood. While sitting out on the course, Eastwood mentioned that he would begin shooting his latest movie in just two days, which also happened to be his 88th birthday. Shocked at the boundless energy of this man, Toby Keith asked Eastwood, "How do you keep on going like this?"

Without hesitation, Clint Eastwood said, "Every morning I just get up and go on. I don't let the old man in."

This advice was so inspirational that over the next few months, Toby Keith wrote the famous song titled with the same mantra. *"Don't Let the Old Man In"* became a hit ballad for Keith and was even used in the same movie that Eastwood had mentioned during their golf outing. As the chorus of the song goes, "When he rides up on his horse, and you feel that cold, bitter wind, look out your window and smile—don't let the old man in."

Clint Eastwood understands that creaky bones, declining health, and the many challenges of old age are going to come knocking on his door every single day. But he refuses to allow them to control his life or steer him off course from his destiny.

And he's right! A critical step in having joy in your later years is by refusing to let yourself become like those dry wineskins that are no longer useful to God's kingdom. At each and every stage in life, God wants to do something new. He has a place and a purpose for you in this very season. Don't let the old you move back in.

* * *

In closing: Stop living in the past. Don't run back to a season from twenty years ago. Move beyond the world that once was. Live each day in the present—which is your gift, from God.

Trust the Lord to bring opportunities to mentor and share your wisdom with others. And, pray for them.

Keep yourself active and your mind sharp. Make plans for the next ten years and commit them to God. Include time to play and time to pray.

Be mindful of the situations you have to serve others in ministry. Stay the course.

And most importantly, expect to leave a legacy of faith with those in your care.

Now, who is ready to join me in climbing out of this old box?

CONCLUSION

CONCLUSION

THE PASSING ON OF WISDOM

If I could leave one piece of advice for the upcoming generations, it would be?

The list below features the most popular answers to this question, as provided by hundreds of people, age 55 and over. They are common-sense views on concepts such as how to spend your time and money, things you wish you had known, being true to oneself and taking things lightly.

Psalms 22:30 says, "Future generations will hear of the wonders of the Lord." If these ideas were conveyed to and received by upcoming generations, they would positively impact the health, wealth, and self of every individual.

As you've learned, wisdom is partially derived from experience. This advice reflects the disappointments following failure and the confidence gained from success. While you may not agree with every recommendation given, there are likely a few points that will make you shout, "Amen!"

Be inspired as you review the wisdom that older Americans hope to impart on the future.

- Enjoy being young!
- Stay true.
- Work hard and take more vacations.
- Save for retirement.
- Respect the earth, with all of its wonders.
- Retire A.S.A.P.
- Approach life at full speed ahead!
- Carpè Diem (and save early and consistently!)

- Be productive. It's all about building understanding, your ability to do things, and accomplishing useful goals.
- Life won't be fair.
- Don't trash the world.
- Be good.
- Slow down.
- Live life to the fullest.
- Change the world, for good!
- Think about what's essential in your life and pay attention to it.
- Be comfortable about yourself and do what you can to stay healthy.
- Always follow your heart, and you will have less regret later in life.
- Think for yourself and always trust that gut feeling!
- Invest early and live below your means.
- Living for Jesus is all the reward you will need.
- Be strong in heart, mind, and soul. And, be honest with yourself.
- Follow your dreams, and no one else's.
- Always have a positive outlook!
- Your golden years are from age 30 to 50.
- Work for yourself.
- Integrity is the key to success and happiness.
- Do not blame others—stay in control of your own life.
- Save. Don't spend!
- Do the right thing by others.
- Be open-minded.
- Never regret; try everything.
- Cooperate.
- Don't take anything for granted.
- Stop whining about everything!

- There isn't such a thing as a free lunch; take care of your own, and then you will be able to take care of others.
- Don't wait. Do it now!
- Respect those who came before you.
- Take care of your elders. They need you, even if they don't admit it.
- Don't let other cultures control yours.
- Seek a relationship with Jesus. You will go on the most incredible adventure of your life.
- Continue to learn new technologies, but also appreciate and learn from the experiences of prior generations.
- Be dedicated and committed to whatever you do. And be proud of it!
- Stay healthy!
- Get as much education as you can. It's something that can never be taken away from you. And, you can change the world with that knowledge.
- Enjoy your friends and family.
- Get off your lazy tail and work!
- Don't hate. Learn to leave things alone.
- Put your trust and hope completely in Jesus!
- Wear sunscreen.
- Get involved!
- Buy land.
- Get a good job. Remember: Being self-employed isn't for everyone!
- Travel.
- There is dignity in hard work.
- Vote!
- Stay positive.
- Read the real history and think before accepting today's distortion of it!
- Enjoy every day and make wise choices.

- Take care of the planet.
- Don't get addicted to a relationship.
- Attend trade school, not college.
- Don't rely on Social Security.
- Put God first!
- Don't lie; be honest.
- Listen to those older than you. They have knowledge that you can benefit from.
- God is the same yesterday, today, and forever. Don't leave Him out of decisions because you think His Word is outdated.
- The older you get, the more you realize, the less you actually know. Stay humble and open.
- Moisturize!
- Be at peace with yourself and others.
- Be more dignified.
- Enter the military for at least two years.
- Think about "things" more significant than yourself!
- Save, save, save.
- Pray for God's guidance and surround yourself with Christian family and friends.
- Don't screw it up!
- Don't just go through the motions of marriage, kids, and career. Enjoy them. As mundane as some of those moments are, you'll never get them back!
- Say "I'm sorry," even if you're not at fault.
- Say "I love you" always.
- Trust that God has your back every step of the way. Don't ever waver from that.
- Don't get so caught up in the details that you lose your joy.
- Laugh every day, even when you may feel pain.
- Learn from history. It will repeat itself if you don't learn and change.

- This world is changing every day and not always for good. Always know God is by your side and is there for you.
- Make your days count!
- Become best friends with Jesus.
- Don't sweat the small stuff; don't fret those things you can't control.
- Make goals for yourself; write them down and check them off.
- Take care of your body.
- Turn off the news!
- Surround yourself with honorable friends.
- Value your life and the legacy you will leave.
- Personal relationships are more important than your paycheck.
- Love one another through the ups and downs. Life isn't easy. Love is what lasts and matters.
- Do your best each and every day.
- Never compromise your core values.
- Don't compare yourself to others. Everyone has their own journey to seek.
- Cherish every moment as a gift from God.
- Live in the now!

CONCLUSION

WHERE DO YOU GO FROM HERE?

No man is ever the same after God has laid His hand upon him. A. W. TOZER

I WOULD BE REMISS to close this book without offering every reader the opportunity to give their heart to Jesus. The Bible makes it clear that this mortal life is only temporary. As a child of God, you were created to live in eternity with Him.

But going to church all of your life or reading a book on Christianity doesn't ensure that you will go to Heaven. There is only one way to Heaven, and that is through acceptance of Jesus Christ as your Lord and Savior. No one comes to the Father God, except through Jesus. As you enter your later years on this earth, it is more important than ever that you consider where you will spend the rest of eternity.

And it's not just about life in the hereafter. It's about now. Are you at peace with God? There is a hole in every human heart that only He can fill. If you're trying to find peace through other means, it won't come except through Him.

If you picked up this book, not knowing that it was written from a Christian perspective, you might not understand that God has a plan just for you—and it's a good plan. John 10:10 says that Jesus came that we might have *life* and life more *abundantly*. Not just abundance in the sweet by and by. But here, in the now!

Allow the Lord into your heart this day. Receive His forgiveness for past sins. Receive His reconciliation for past mistakes and broken dreams. Receive His peace for that longing in your heart. And most important, receive His best plan for the days that remain.

Just say, "Lord Jesus, I repent of my sins. I ask you to come into my heart. I make you my Lord and Savior." It's a simple prayer, but a powerful one that will change your life now and forever.

I'm praying for you and believing that God will bring everything you need to find joy and purpose in the later seasons of your life.

CONCLUSION

A PRAYER OF BLESSING FOR MIDDLE AGE

DEAR LORD, thank You for this day—the day which You have made. No matter the circumstances for today, I will rejoice and be glad in it. I believe that Your face is smiling toward me. Reveal Your love to me so that I may share it with others.

Thank you for my past, my present, and my future. I'm grateful for the many blessings You have poured into my life. And I believe that Your blessings will extend through me to a thousand generations.

I know that You still have a plan for me. Teach me how to live today according to Your purpose and not be distracted by the noise of this world. I choose to fix my eyes ahead and not look back to the past.

Going forward, allow the trials I have walked through to become a testimony for others. Give me opportunities to mentor people who need to be encouraged or those who need a vision of victory for their own life. Help me to declare Your Word over my life, and over the lives of those around me.

Bring wisdom to me, Lord, through my experiences and through the knowledge You've given me. I surrender all of my unfulfilled dreams and unmet expectations. I purpose to forget what lies behind. You are a God of restoration. I believe that You will take every obstacle in my life and turn it into a blessing. This is a new day, and You are taking me to a new level.

You're a good, good Father. And no good thing will You withhold from those whose walk is blameless. Like Paul, I choose to press toward the mark for the prize of the high calling of God in Jesus Christ.

Give me the courage to walk in Your ways. Give me faith to trust You with all of the unknowns on the path that lies before me. Fill my thoughts with Your thoughts.

Thank You that You desire above all things that I prosper and be in good health, even as my soul prospers. Allow me to rest in Your goodness Lord, as You restore my soul. I surrender my mind, will, and emotions to You, and trust in the mercy of Your Holy Spirit to minister peace, forgiveness, and wholeness to my life. I am a new creation in Christ.

I will meditate daily on Your promises. And, according to Your Word, I declare today that my future is blessed and cannot be cursed. No weapon formed against me will prosper.

I have everything I need for the rest of my days. I am healthy. I am restored. I am an overcomer.

I am a child of the Most High God. I am safe, for You have appointed legions of angels to watch over me and care for me. Your favor surrounds me as a shield. I am never far from Your sight.

You are Jehovah Nissi, my banner. You are Jehovah Shalom, my peace. You are Jehovah Rapha, my healer. You are Jehovah, Jireh, my provider. You are Jehovah Shammah, my ever-present light in the darkness. I call upon Your name. I trust in Your name and in the power of Your Word.

I declare by faith that my best days are ahead.

In Jesus' name. Amen.

ABOUT THE AUTHOR

TERESA GRANBERRY is a wife, mom, and proud Gigi to her seven grandchildren. She comes from the unique perspective of being the granddaughter, daughter, stepdaughter, and wife of former ministers of the Gospel.

When she was a young woman, her family was in a tragic car accident after being hit head-on by a drunk driver. Teresa was thrown through the back window of the car and suffered numerous injuries. But amazingly, her life and health were spared. She felt the call of the Lord to spread the love of Jesus while in the hospital ICU.

She is the founder of Harvest Creek Ministry by Design, a ministry that teaches women how to host Christ in their home and in their hearts.

www.ingramcontent.com/pod-product-compliance
Lightning Source LLC
Chambersburg PA
CBHW071400290426
44108CB00014B/1632